The
POWER
of the
RING

Endorsements of *The Power of the Ring* . . .

"If anyone asks me what one book about Tolkien is the most worth reading, *The Power of the Ring* is my reply."
—Peter Kreeft, Boston College

"A literally wonderful—wonder-full—book. It will open the eyes of any reader who considers *The Lord of the Rings* just a gripping yarn in a fantasy world. Tolkien's 'vision' (Caldecott makes it clear the word is just right) draws on deep springs of philosophy and mysticism— and, not least, the orthodoxy of the church." **—Aidan Nichols, O.P.**

"Stratford Caldecott, who has been delighting discerning readers for years with his sparkling writings on religious and spiritual subjects, has produced a masterful guide to the works of J. R. R. Tolkien. Finally the Christian riches of *The Lord of the Rings, The Silmarillion, The Hobbit*, and Tolkien's other masterpieces shine forth for all to enjoy. An indispensable guide to the most popular author of modern times." **—Philip Zaleski, editor, The Best Spiritual Writing series**

"This book contains profound insights into the theology and spirituality in Tolkien's books. Caldecott gives the background of Tolkien's personality, letters, excerpts from other writings in order to provide a clear picture of what's at work in the *Lord of the Rings*. The chapter 'Behind the Stars' is among the deepest commentaries on JRRT's work as a whole. Very fine. Definitely worth owning."
—Peter A. Kwasniewski, Wyoming Catholic College

"Professor Tolkien, the academic philologist, was said to have travelled 'inside language'. Under Caldecott's guidance, here we travel inside the language of Tolkien. One sees at last what he was up to. It is a revelatory book."   **—*Church Times***

"Every Catholic school will want a copy as will anyone interested in Tolkien as a serious writer."   **—Eric Hester, *The Catholic Times***

"This book will be welcomed by those interested in the deep theological underpinnings of Tolkien's works, and is recommended to academic libraries supporting upper level coursework on Tolkien or religion and literature."—**Daniel Boice, *Catholic Library World***

"Essential reading for those who would like to understand the spiritual background to *Lord of the Rings*."
                    —*Scientific and Medical Network*

To the servants of
the Secret fire

The
POWER
of the
RING

The Spiritual Vision Behind
The Hobbit and *The Lord of the Rings*

STRATFORD CALDECOTT

A Crossroad Book
The Crossroad Publishing Company
New York

The Crossroad Publishing Company
831 Chestnut Ridge Road
Chestnut Ridge, NY 10977
www.crossroadpublishing.com

Second Edition

This book is a revised and expanded edition of *Secret Fire: The Spiritual Vision of J. R. R. Tolkien* (London: Darton, Longman & Todd, 2003) and a revised second edition of *The Power of the Ring: The Spiritual Vision behind* The Lord of the Rings (New York: Crossroad, 2005). It also includes revisions that were made for a Russian edition in 2007.

In continuation of our 200-year tradition of independent publishing, The Crossroad Publishing Company proudly offers a variety of books with strong, original voices and diverse perspectives. The viewpoints expressed in our books are not necessarily those of The Crossroad Publishing Company, any of its imprints or of its employees. No claims are made or responsibility assumed for any health or other benefit.

The text of this book is set in Utopia. The display faces are ITC Zapf Chancery and Morris Troy. The stylized crossed letter C logo is a registered trademark of The Crossroad Publishing Company.

Printed in the United States of America

———————————————

Project Management by
The Crossroad Publishing Company
Maggie Pate Duffey

Cover Art: Ted Nasmith
Cover Design: Ray Lundgren
Page Layout: John Eagleson

ISBN: 978-0-8245-4983-1
Library of Congress Control Number: 2012920468

Contents

Acknowledgments

Special thanks are due to my family, including my Elvish wife, Léonie, and our daughters, Tessa, Sophie, and Rosie. (Tessa's own independent research on Tolkien was awe-inspiring.) To my mother, the novelist and folklorist Moyra Caldecott, I owe my appreciation of myth and story. My father, Oliver, was one of the publishers of *The Lord of the Rings* in the early 1960s, and it was thanks to him that I began to read and love it. I am also grateful to Carol and Phil Zaleski for their helpful comments on a draft of the book, and to Yvonne Aburrow for a fascinating discussion of modern Paganism. Fr. Ian Boyd, C.S.B., published several of my articles on Tolkien in the *Chesterton Review* and has kindly given permission to reuse some of that material here. One of those articles was given as the first in a series of Tolkien Lectures at Bath Spa University under the auspices of the chaplain, Fr. William McLoughlin, O.S.M., and subsequently also appeared as "The Heroism of Hobbits" in *Hidden Presence: The Catholic Imagination of J. R. R. Tolkien* (Chesterton Press, 2003). Another paper, "The Lord and Lady of the Rings," was published in *Touchstone* magazine and on the associated website. This and any other recycled material used in the present book has been thoroughly reworked. Inklings admirers in England, America, Spain, and Italy have provided me with many other opportunities to expand my appreciation of Tolkien. I am grateful to the Tolkien Estate for permission to reproduce extracts (though far fewer than I would have wished) from the works of Tolkien himself. Finally, I want to thank the many readers who bought the first edition of this book and thus encouraged the publisher to let me expand it for a new edition (most authors never get such a chance!). Thanks in particular to Gwendolin Herder for making this possible. I must apologize to those original readers who may now feel tempted to buy this improved (I hope definitive) version in place of the one they already own.

Preface to the Revised Edition

The book is about Tolkien's spirituality, by which I mean his religious awareness and experience, the things he believed about life and death and ultimate truth. Tolkien was a devout Christian, a Roman Catholic. But somehow he managed to write a book that appeals equally to Christian and to Pagan readers, and to people who have no particular beliefs but simply love reading a good fantasy adventure story. As a result, his readership is extremely broad. But whenever a lot of people come to love a particular author, they also love to get together to share their affection and to discuss the books that inspire them so much. *The Lord of the Rings* gives rise to societies and clubs, and even to academic conferences and journals, dedicated to the study of Tolkien's works. Secondary works, like this one, are written to help others to understand the writer and his background.

But what is it about Tolkien's works that inspire a particular, almost spiritual devotion? When Viggo Mortenson, the actor who played Aragorn in the film trilogy by Peter Jackson, was asked why *The Lord of the Rings* was so popular, he replied, "Because it is a true story." In other words, it is not *merely* a fantasy, but communicates something that is true, something that people feel and recognize as important for their own lives. That is why I wrote this book—as an attempt to show some of the "truth" that can be found in Tolkien's writing. It is not about *historical* truth, despite the fact that the author made the history of Middle-earth remarkably convincing. It is not even about *philological* truth, or the truth (which was Tolkien's professional concern at Oxford) concerning the real origins and meanings of the words in our language. The truth it is really about is more subtle and much deeper than that. It is a truth about the way people behave, about the moral life of courage and integrity and honesty and the constant battles we have to fight to protect that life. It is also, at an even deeper level, about the reality and value of beauty.

There are many kinds of beauty, and Tolkien portrays them in his stories: the homely beauty of firelight and good cheer, the rich natural beauty of tree and forest, the awesome majesty of mountains, the charm of the babbling stream, the terrifying spectacle of the ever-changing sea, the high and remote glimmer of the stars. All of them are important to him, as they should be to us, but he gives a special place to the high and remote, the heart-piecing beauty of starlight, and the call of the seagulls over the ocean, associating these with the elves and with the Elvish strain in human nature. They recall for him the mystery that lies beyond the beauties of this world, and awaken a longing in the human heart that will never be quite content in Middle-earth. We know that no earthly beauty can survive death, and so in the midst of our happiness in this life (though we may forget it and should forget it from time to time, as the Hobbits do at bath-time or around a mug of beer with friends) there is a sadness or a yearning that is precious to us and not to be denied. Deep within us, and high above the clouds, we sense that there is something yet to be revealed, some face, some word, something we cannot ever fully grasp. This thing that Tolkien sought and expressed, and to which his friend C. S. Lewis gave the name Joy, is everywhere present in *The Lord of the Rings* like a kind of atmosphere, or the tingling freshness of mountain water, and this is why so many of us love to read the story over and over again. It is like breathing fresh air.

There are other ways in which *The Lord of the Rings* is a "true story," or illuminates some aspect of the real world. Tolkien always denied that the War of the Ring should be read as a veiled description either of the Second World War or of the First. Nevertheless, he agreed that the story might be "applicable" to those and many other wars, and to other situations. I explore how the Ring can serve as a symbol for sin, for pride, for machinery, and for power. Tolkien's son Christopher fought in a war against a dictator whose psychology bears some resemblance to that of Saruman, and whose last moments must have resembled Denethor's. There are plenty of lessons to be learned from Tolkien's story about the inner corruption of those who seek to control the wills of others, albeit at first for ends which seem to them perfectly noble. Once having read the story, one will be able the better to recognize certain kinds of commonplace evil in the outside world.

Tolkien's popularity is undeniable. There is considerable academic interest in the languages he created and the complex and subtle ways he incorporated, reworked, and transformed the various mythologies of Europe and Scandinavia. There is growing awareness, since the publication of this letters, of the religious and Catholic underpinning of his mythology. But none of this yet touches on his real importance. We cannot claim for Tolkien's writing a perfection of form and content that would place it alongside that of Dante or Shakespeare. The *legendarium* was in any case largely unfinished. But no matter what its imperfections may be, it is a great blow struck against the tendency to imagine the world as flat, meaningless, and spiritless, and human beings as mere animals governed by chance and instinct. It awakens in us the sense that we are interiorly free. Moral goodness is present, indeed supreme, in Tolkien's saga. For although history is a long defeat, with each seeming golden age containing the seeds of its own destruction, history is also a long victory for those who are prepared to follow the light wherever it leads. For even if it leads through darkness, "Day will come again." Tolkien's characters, in victory or defeat, speak to us of hope (*Estel*), a hope that evil cannot quench because it is kindled from the Secret Fire.

STRATFORD CALDECOTT
secondspring.co.uk
Oxford, March 25, 2012

The
POWER
of the
RING

Introduction

The Lord of the Rings is said to have been the most widely read book of the twentieth century after the Bible. An epic fantasy about the quest to destroy an evil Ring of Power, it appeals to people of all ages and beliefs, in a broad spectrum from Christian to neo-Pagan. Its author, an Oxford don, was a devout Roman Catholic, but the majority of his readers are not aware of this. An understanding of J. R. R. Tolkien's personal beliefs and their influence on the story for which he is famous can only enhance our appreciation of this great work of art.

Ever since the Second World War, and certainly since the 1960s, the fashion among our intelligentsia on both sides of the Atlantic has been to expose (or even exaggerate) the all-too-human side of the great and the famous: aristocrats, politicians, artists, explorers, scientists. However, the yearning for real heroism never dies. *The Lord of the Rings* is heroic saga on a grand scale, belonging to an ancient tradition of magical romances and legend. In his review C. S. Lewis paid it this tribute:

> The book is like lightning from a clear sky; as sharply different, as unpredictable in our age as [William Blake's] *Songs of Innocence* were in theirs. To say that in it heroic romance, gorgeous, eloquent, and unashamed, has suddenly returned at a period almost pathological in its anti-romanticism, is inadequate.... It marks not a return but an advance or

1

revolution: the conquest of new territory. Nothing quite like it was ever done before.[1]

The Lord of the Rings was an advance because it was not merely heroic, nor merely romantic. Though permeated with a kind of nostalgia, it was a thoroughly modern work. Literary expert Tom Shippey compares it to the work of William Golding, George Orwell, and T. H. White, all of whom wrote fantasy as a way of struggling with evils that had been exposed by the great twentieth-century wars. Their writing was "modern" because it was deeply marked by this experience. Millions of human beings died on the fields of France, in Russia, in the death camps of Germany, in the fire-bombing of Dresden, in the nuclear conflagration of Hiroshima and Nagasaki. By the time of Tolkien's death in 1973, a moral miasma had settled over the spirits of the English, as the disillusionment and the compromises of the century began to take their toll.

What the book celebrates—and mourns—is a world and a tradition that appear to be passing away in a great war, or series of wars. These wars are fought in a good cause, against an enemy that cannot be allowed to win. Yet the real danger is not that the free world might be defeated; it is that we might be corrupted, brutalized, and degraded by the conflict itself and in particular by the means employed to secure victory. Tolkien always denied that Mordor was intended as a representation of Nazi Germany, or Soviet Russia, but was quite aware of its "applicability" to the death camps and the gulags, to Fascism and Communism—as well as to other, more subtle or fragmentary manifestations of the same spirit.

Of course, the point is partly that the allies against Sauron resisted the temptation to use the Ring against its maker, and as a result the War of the Ring could be the prelude to a new Golden Age in Middle-earth, a civilization of love, justice, and peace. And yet even in the War of the Ring (as the opening of the film version reminds us), much that was beautiful departed and is now forgotten. Our mistake in the great wars of our own time has been to accept the false idea that the end justifies the means, and that "if a thing can be done, it must be done" (*Letters* 186).[2] For, as Tolkien wrote to his son in 1944, the Allies were attempting to defeat Sauron by using the Ring. The penalty would be to breed new Saurons, and to turn Men and elves into orcs—"Not that in real life things are as clear cut as in a story, and we started with a great many orcs on our side" (L 66).

Monsters and Critics

Tolkien's importance as a postwar writer who used fantasy to explore profound moral and spiritual themes was not recognized when *The Lord of the Rings* was first published in the 1950s. Back in 1936, the subtitle of Tolkien's academic paper on *Beowulf*, "The Monsters and the Critics," had half jokingly implied that the literary critics of the Old English poem which Tolkien loved were adversaries of the hero, perhaps even akin to monsters themselves. And so, when *The Lord of the Rings* did appear in print, Tolkien knew pretty much what to expect. In fact, it was derided by a number of critics on both sides of the Atlantic, Edmund Wilson famously describing it as "juvenile trash."

The reason often given for despising the novel was that "good" and "bad" were so clearly delineated that the plot was simplistic and childish. But, as we have just seen, Tolkien was well aware of the complexity and muddle of real life—and yet held his writing to be "realistic," indeed truer to the inner life than most of the supposedly "grown up" novels the critics had in mind.

> Yes, I think the orcs as real a creation as anything in "real-istic" fiction...only in real life they are on both sides, of course. For "romance" has grown out of "allegory," and its wars are still derived from the "inner war" of allegory in which good is on one side and various modes of badness on the other. In real (exterior) life men are on both sides: which means a motley alliance of orcs, beasts, demons, plain natu-rally honest men, and angels. But it does make some differ-ence who are your captains and whether they are orc-like per se! And what it is all about (or thought to be). It is even in this world possible to be (more or less) in the wrong or in the right. (L 71)

Tolkien drew upon a much older tradition of storytelling than the modern novel, with its typically materialistic assump-tions. He was retrieving the art of mythological or *mythopoeic* thinking, which is as old as mankind itself and deeply entwined with our religious sense. The book appeals to universal con-stants in human nature, constants that are reflected in tradi-tional mythology and folklore the world over. Mythological thinking does not provide an "escape" from reality so much as an "intensification" of it, as another fantasy writer (Alan Gar-ner) once rightly said. It is this that in part explains the novel's wide appeal—and also the contempt it aroused among those whose world-view and mindset are closed in advance against all such uses of the imagination.

The Lord of the Rings may be read, therefore, as an excit-ing story that spectacularly revives an almost-extinct literary genre. But it can also be enjoyed in other ways: as an extended meditation on what it means to be English, or as an imaginative response to the experience of modern warfare, or as a moving evocation of the intimate relationship between love and hero-ism. As we shall see, it can be read, too, as an exploration of the roots of human language and consciousness. Most strangely of all, perhaps, it can be viewed as a deliberate experiment in a kind of *time travel* using dreams and "linguistic ghosts" to overcome the limitations of individual memory and experience.

When the first volume of *The Lord of the Rings* was published, Tolkien wrote in trepidation that "I have exposed my heart to be shot at." The themes of his writing are the keys to Tolkien's own deepest concerns, including death and immortality, nostalgia for paradise, creation and creativity, the reality of virtue and sin, the right stewardship of nature, and the moral dangers posed by the possession of technological power. By wrestling with these concerns he created a body of work that is imbued with a profound wisdom—a wisdom that our civilization desperately needs—drawn very largely from the Catholic faith in which he was raised. Of course, he was not writing dogmatic theology, even in the letters and commentaries where he came closest to explaining what he was about. But because he *believed* in the truth of certain dogmas, these acted for him like torches or crystalline lamps that transmit light into dark places. It was with the light they transmitted and what it might reveal that he was concerned in his own work, not directly with the fashioning of the lamps themselves: he was humble enough to leave that to the professionals. His spirituality is that unpretentious "spirituality of the everyday" that we find in many of the most popular Catholic authors, such as Jean-Pierre de Caussade or Thérèse of Lisieux. The hobbits exemplify this humility and everydayness which is at the heart of his writing.

Thus, while the reader is never assumed to be a Christian believer, the cosmological setting of Tolkien's imagined world, along with the creatures and events with which he filled it and the moral laws governing this imagined cosmos, were all intended to be compatible with his beliefs about reality, and in fact provide "pointers" to a Christian world-view. Love, courage, justice, mercy, kindness, integrity, and the other virtues are incarnated in the story through characters such as Aragorn and Frodo. It is a testimony to the power and realism of the Christian tradition that exposure to these patterns of the moral life can have a purifying effect on the receptive reader, yet without making us feel confined or oppressed within an ideological system. Many of us return to *The Lord of the Rings* again and again for refreshment of soul—perhaps even for the kind of healing that the author must have experienced in the writing of it.

My exploration of Tolkien's vision will draw upon the stories themselves, including his popular earlier novel for children, *The Hobbit*, and several important short stories, along with the *History of Middle-Earth,* edited from Tolkien's papers by his son Christopher, but also upon the published *Letters*, Tolkien's own essays, short stories, and poems, and some of the best critical and biographical works that have appeared in the last few years. The dedication and the title of the first Part of this book hardly need explaining to anyone who has read *The Lord of the Rings*, or seen the Peter Jackson movie. Gandalf the wizard names himself a "servant of the Secret Fire" during his confrontation with the balrog in Moria, and he is in fact later revealed as the bearer of the Elvish Ring of Fire, Narya the Great. But the fire he serves is not simply that of the ring he bears. Fire is a much bigger and more complex theme in the stories than that. Indeed, the secret fire is at the heart not just of *The Lord of the Rings* but of the wider tapestry of stories sometimes known as "the *legendarium*" or "the Silmarillion" (I will use the latter in italics only when I am referring to the published book of that title). Only the fire in Mount Doom, where the One Ring was forged, is capable of destroying it. The power of that fire, earthly though it is, proves greater than the power of the Ring, but behind it stands a greater power still. Let us now go in search of Tolkien's secret fire, which the Enemy also sought but failed to find, "for it is with Ilúvatar."

Part One

THE SECRET FIRE

Chapter One

The Tree of Tales

Tolkien was an explorer. The stories in which he invested so much time and energy are notes of his expeditions in search of an older or "inner" world. Over the years he added revision after revision, layer by layer, often working late into the night, filling in a vast historical canvas, weaving theme upon theme, until the whole collection resembled a great "tree of tales," like the gnarled oaks he loved.

Now that we have access to the vast corpus of unfinished and reworked stories and background material, thanks to his son Christopher's labors on the twelve-volume *History of Middle-Earth*, we can see how much time and energy went into this writing. If his contemporaries and peers had known the full scale of his enterprise, they would have been shocked. What drove Tolkien so late into the night was not merely the obsession to tell a story, but the belief that "legends and myths are largely made of 'truth,' and indeed present aspects of it that can only be perceived in this mode" (L 131). He knew he was writing fiction, but at the same time he felt that he was *telling the truth* about the world as it revealed itself to him. And this truth he discovered as he wrote, through the very process of writing. He claimed always to have had the sense that he was recording what was already "there," rather than inventing stuff out of his own head (L 131), a feeling that lay behind the fictional device of the "Red Book of Westmarch" on which *The Lord of the Rings* itself pretended to be based. In a letter to Christopher he admitted that the story seemed almost to write

11

itself and sometimes took a direction very different from the preliminary sketch, as if the truth was trying to emerge through him (L 91). In some sense, then, he did actually believe what he was writing. ("There are secondary planes or degrees," he writes in the "Notion Club Papers.")

His stories were set not in a distant galaxy or another world, but in this world a long time ago. In a draft letter to an admirer dated 1971 (L 328), Tolkien described writing with great care for detail, so as to produce a "picture" that would appear to be set against a limitless background, with infinite extensions through both time and space. Each particular element of the story had to appear to belong to a much larger and more ancient body of literature, in order to evoke the symbolic resonances without which it would fail to cast its spell. There had to be a sense of great vistas around and behind each story, as there is in the legends of a people like the Norsemen or the Celts, each of which comes down to us out of its own tremendous "mythic space."

But what follows in the same letter is especially interesting. It seems to suggest that, while he could analyze to some extent what he was doing and why, and how he achieved the literary effects he did, he was at the same time extremely puzzled by what had been give to him—that he felt a mystery at work. He goes on:

> Looking back on the wholly unexpected things that have followed its publication ... I feel as if an ever darkening sky over our present world had been suddenly pierced, the clouds rolled back, and an almost forgotten sunlight had poured down again. As if indeed the horns of Hope had been heard again, as Pippin heard them suddenly at the absolute *nadir* of the fortunes of the West. But *How?* and *Why?* (L 328)

The Tree of Tales

This sense of mystery is deepened by an encounter in real life with a figure he identifies as Gandalf, in the person of a man who visited him to discuss certain old pictures that seemed almost designed to illustrate *The Lord of the Rings*, but which Tolkien had never before seen. The man remarks after a silence: "Of course you don't suppose, do you, that you wrote all that book yourself?" Tolkien goes on:

> Pure Gandalf! I was too well acquainted with G. to expose myself rashly, or to ask what he meant. I think I said: "No, I don't suppose so any longer." I have never since been able to suppose so. An alarming conclusion for an old philologist to draw concerning his private amusement. But not one that should puff any one up who considers the imperfections of "chosen instruments," and indeed what sometimes seems their lamentable unfitness for the purpose.

A "chosen instrument"? I don't want to make too much of this, but the letter is revealing, especially in light of his early sense of mission, discussed in John Garth's book (see Bibliography). Tolkien seems to have felt that it had been given to him to sound the horn of hope in a darkling world, and those many thousands of readers who return again and again to the book and film for refreshment of soul might well agree with him. This is a story that tells us things we need to know. It cannot be taken in all at once. It is one of those that we have to *grow into,* stories that deal with the way the world is made and the way the self is made. These stories are like dreams, but dreams that can be shared by an entire culture; wholesome dreams that restore a balance to the psyche by turning our energies and our thoughts toward truth; dreams that resemble an oasis in the desert. Reading them can be a meditation. Why is that? This is the question I want to answer.

The Hall of Fire

J. R. R. Tolkien was born in Bloemfontein, South Africa, in 1892 and lived there until the age of three. Then for reasons of health his mother, Mabel, brought him and his younger brother Hilary back to England, for what was intended originally to be a temporary visit; but his father, Arthur, who was supposed to join them later, died before the family were reunited, and Mabel settled with the children at Sarehole, a beautiful corner of rural Warwickshire just outside Birmingham.

When Mabel became a Roman Catholic in 1900, she was cut off from the support of her mixed Anglican, Baptist, and Unitarian family and reduced to poverty. She was forced to move from the countryside into the town, and there she was taken under the wing of Father Francis Morgan, C.O., a priest of the Oratory of St. Philip Neri in Birmingham, a religious community whose English branch had been founded by John Henry Newman fifty years earlier. It was Fr. Morgan who helped to look after the family financially and provided their main source of spiritual guidance.

Tolkien was only twelve when his mother died of diabetes, worn out (he later wrote) by the poverty that was a direct result of her conversion to Catholicism, and Fr. Morgan became the boy's guardian. Thus it was that he grew to manhood under the protection and guidance of an exemplary Catholic priest. Most of his life he tried to attend Mass daily, finding in it a constant source of strength and grace.

Thereafter the story of his life might be presented under three main headings. The first of these would be *Romance*. He falls in love at the age of sixteen with the nineteen-year-old Edith Bratt, but is not allowed by his priest-guardian to propose to her until he comes of age five years later. Edith having consented to be received into the Catholic Church, they are married in Warwick just before Tolkien sets off with the Lancashire Fusiliers to fight the Germans in the First World War. Only when he returns are they able to live happily as man and wife. The image he has of her is always that of a young beauty dancing among the hemlocks in a forest glade near Roos in Yorkshire, close to the military camp where Tolkien was stationed in 1917: it is one of the seeds of his writing, for it becomes the encounter between his hero Beren and the Elven princess Lúthien—echoed also in the story of Aragorn and Arwen which, though it is mainly found in the Appendices of *The Lord of the Rings*, Tolkien regarded as a vital element of the story.

Heading number two: *War*. The earliest beginnings of the written mythology date from 1914, the year Britain entered the First World War, although Tolkien is allowed to finish his studies at Oxford in 1915 before beginning his full-time military training. He survives the war through the "luck" of being sent back from the Somme with trench fever. As he recovers, he writes the first sustained fragment of the Silmarillion, "The Fall of Gondolin." Most of his male friends are killed within a few years, and he is awed by the heroism of the ordinary English soldier. That heroism will find its way into *The Lord of the Rings*, into the Hobbits, and the figure of Sam Gamgee in particular. Published in 1954–55, the whole novel is a tribute to the spirit of ordinary, decent men who died for their country in the Great War, and it is largely composed during the Second World War, in the face of the later, almost demonic evil unleashed on the world by Adolf Hitler.

The third heading is *Oxford*, where Tolkien (after five years teaching in Leeds) becomes Professor of Anglo-Saxon in 1925, and forms the Kolbitár (Coalbiter) reading group devoted to the Icelandic sagas. He later becomes part of the Inklings group that formed around C. S. Lewis after 1933. The influence of this real-life fellowship on his writing cannot be overestimated: without it he would have lacked the encouragement or confidence to continue. The friendship of Lewis in particular (another survivor of the trenches), whom he helped to convert to Christianity in 1931 after a late-night conversation in the grounds of Magdalen College, played a crucial role, as did that of George Sayer, who at one point revived his determination to find a publisher.

Much has been written on the Inklings over the years, as the fame of Lewis and Tolkien spread around the world, not least an important study by Humphrey Carpenter, Tolkien's biographer. I will not try to summarize it all here: as with the details of Tolkien's life, the facts are easily available. Though Tolkien influenced Lewis's conversion to Christianity, the latter never became a Catholic. The other members of the group were an even more varied bunch, ranging from Charles Williams, the High-Church Anglican with his mystical and somewhat unorthodox ideas about love and magic, to Owen Barfield, the Anthroposophist with an interest in language and the evolution of consciousness. Anyone who has lived in Oxford and attended the pubs where the group often met will be able to picture the scene—pints of bitter wreathed in smoke, loud conversation (especially from Lewis), ancient languages, fragments of story and new poems intoned, frequent interruptions, critical comment, and laughter.

I sometimes think of the Inklings (not to mention the "Coalbiters"!) when I read the description of Elrond's "Hall of Fire" in Rivendell, for it is there that they would have been most at home. The hall was a constant element in Tolkien's writing, its first appearance being the Room of the Log Fire in a story he wrote back in 1916–17 called "The Cottage of Lost

Play," where "old tales, old songs, and elfin music are treasured and rehearsed."

It is easy to idealize the Inklings, but the reality was often humdrum enough, with its fair share of frustration and human weakness. It was an informal group, and members came and went. In the end even Tolkien and Lewis fell out somewhat, partly over Lewis's marriage to a divorcée, to which Tolkien, as a devout Catholic, took exception. Perhaps, as some allege, there may have been some jealousy on Tolkien's part of Lewis's apparently easy success with the Narnia stories, which he thought rather clumsy and allegorical (L 265), and of Lewis's close friendship with Charles Williams (this by his own admission in L 252, 257, 259).

Nevertheless, the friendships among "the brotherhood" were real and deep, and many moments of intense communion more than made up for the occasional tensions. Lewis never ceased to praise Tolkien's work, even during the period of estrangement, and for his part Tolkien was deeply shaken by Lewis's death in 1963, writing: "this feels like an axe-blow near the roots. Very sad that we should have been so separated in the last years; but our time of close communion endured in memory for both of us" (L 251). For many years, Lewis had been Tolkien's only audience for what might have remained, but for this, a private hobby (L 276).

Although *The Lord of the Rings* may have depended on the encouragement of Lewis (combined with the success of Tolkien's children's story *The Hobbit*) to get it going, the secret life that was to feed into it was well under way before the Inklings ever started to read to each other in the Eagle and Child—the Oxford pub they called the "Bird and Baby"—and long before Tolkien wrote the famous academic essays that summed up his thoughts on literature: "Beowulf: The Monsters and the

Critics" (1936) and "On Fairy-Stories" (1939). It was under way even before the war that had marked him permanently with the experience of great evil and suffering. The seeds of that secret life lie back in his childhood, and especially in the happy days he spent playing with his brother Hilary in the countryside around Sarehole (the inspiration for Hobbiton) and in the intimations of "beauty and majesty" he received on a daily basis in the Catholic Mass.

Going "Inside Language"

From his earliest introduction to Church Latin by his mother he loved languages, and quickly began to make up some of his own. Through the study of languages, a whole range of other influences began to reach him. Eventually Tolkien was to master many European tongues, both ancient and modern, but he always retained a particular affection for Latin, Gothic, Welsh, and Finnish. He loved poetry more than prose, probably because it expressed the rhythms and character of each language in purest form. The "Sister Songs" of the mystical Victorian Catholic poet Francis Thompson may have helped kindle his love of elves, but in 1912 he began to study Finnish, and here he tells us he found the seeds of Quenya, the High-Elvish of his own invention. He once wrote to W. H. Auden of the pleasure he experienced reading a Finnish Grammar in Exeter College library, when he was supposed to be preparing for an exam: "It was like discovering a complete wine cellar filled with bottles of an amazing wine of a kind and flavor never tasted before" (L 163).

It was the mystique of Northern Europe (which he sometimes called "Northernness") that particularly appealed to him, a spirit that he felt in the Norse or Icelandic sagas, for example the "Prophecy of the Seeress" in the *Elder Edda* concerning the beginning and end of the world. He believed that the mythology of his own land in particular had been lost or destroyed (or overlayed by Celtic and French influences). It needed to be recovered in something of the way Nikolaj Grundtvig had compiled the Danish and Norwegian legends and the Grimm brothers the "Teutonic" in the nineteenth century, or Snorri Sturluson the Icelandic in the thirteenth. These men had been, like Tolkien, Christians trying to preserve what they saw as enriching or beautiful in Pagan material.

Just as influential, and very much an inspiration to Tolkien, was Elias Lönnrot, a Lutheran Christian who reconstituted Finnish folklore from surviving oral and runic traditions during the nineteenth century. It is generally agreed that Lönnrot's *Kalevala* played a crucial role in the development of Finnish national identity, consolidated when Finland achieved independence at the end of 1917. Rudolf Steiner, the founder of the Anthroposophical Society and a major influence on Owen Barfield, lectured on the *Kalevala* in Helsinki in 1912, believing it to be one of Europe's great sacred texts, the vehicle of a secret wisdom. For Tolkien it represented the possibility of a "good Paganism" compatible with Christianity. Probably in the same year that Steiner was lecturing, Tolkien began to work on the *Kalevala* and to adapt some of its themes and characters into stories of his own (the tragic hero Kullervo, mingled with Sigurd and Oedipus from other sources, became Túrin in *Unfinished Tales*).

Then there was Anglo-Saxon. This was the language that had come to maturity in eighth-century Northumbria, at the confluence of two movements of Christian missionaries, from north and south: the Celtic monks from Ireland and Iona to Lindisfarne, and the Benedictines from Canterbury to York, Wearmouth, and Jarrow. For two golden centuries, before the devastation wrought by the Vikings, a Christian civilization blossomed in the north of England that proved capable of assimilating the best traditions of Paganism and raising them to a new cultural level. The monasteries were islands or oases of culture, producing great works of art like the Lindisfarne Gospels, with their earthy humor and sinuous, interlaced decoration. The English language of that time achieved a maturity that is exemplified by great works such as the *Dream of the Rood* and, of course, *Beowulf*, which Tolkien translated and on which he wrote his most influential scholarly essay. One commentator (Bradley J. Birzer) has likened these monasteries, with their great libraries and lore-masters, such as the Venerable Bede and Alcuin (who became the "schoolmaster of Europe" under Charlemagne), to Rivendell and Lothlórien, and Gandalf to the Anglo-Saxon missionary St. Boniface, defending civilization from the barbarians of the East.

By 1914 Tolkien had encountered a poem of this period by Cynewulf called *Crist* ("Christ"). Two lines of the poem struck him in a way he never forgot:

> *Éalá Éarendel engla beorhtast*
> *ofer middangeard monnum sended!*

> Hail Earendel, brightest of angels,
> above the middle-earth sent unto men!

Tolkien describes the first impact of the poem upon him in the voice of the character Lowdham in his "Notion Club Papers" (about which more below):

> When I came across that citation in the dictionary I felt a curious thrill, as if something had stirred in me, half wakened from sleep. There was something very remote and strange and beautiful behind those words, if I could grasp it,

far beyond ancient English. . . . I don't think it is any irreverence to say that it may derive its curiously moving quality from some older world.

Tolkien, like Lowdham in the story, went in search of that older world. He believed certain vivid dreams could grant access to it. (He often mentions a recurrent "Atlantis dream" of an ineluctable wave drowning a green landscape, which he remembers from his earliest years in South Africa, and which one of his sons also later experienced.) The other way back to the past was through language itself, and "linguistic ghosts" that are traces and vestiges of the ancient world in modern speech or names. At the end of his life, the obituary composed for the *Times* some years earlier by C. S. Lewis described Tolkien as having traveled in some sense "inside language." It is a powerful phrase, and a true one. Verlyn Flieger records the question put to Tolkien once by a fellow philologist: "You broke the veil, didn't you, and passed through?" He "readily admitted" having done so. For him language itself had an interior: by penetrating within it, he found himself entering the same imaginal world to which his special dreams were pointing. In fact, the "older world" is a world both ancient and interior, which is precisely what we mean by *mythic*.

By the end of the long vacation of 1914, Tolkien was staying at Phoenix Farm in Nottinghamshire. There he wrote a poem, the first fruit of his meditations on the mysterious verse from Cynewulf. It was called "The Voyage of Earendel the Evening Star," and it was the beginning of all that is most original in Tolkien's mythology.[3] You will find the most developed form of it at the heart of *The Fellowship of the Ring*: it is the song composed by Bilbo (with a little help from Aragorn) that Frodo hears, half in a dream, in the Hall of Fire in Elrond's house, and it begins as follows:

> Eärendil was a mariner
> that tarried in Arvernien;
> he built a boat of timber felled
> in Nimbrethil to journey in;
> her sails he wove of silver fair,
> of silver were her lanterns made,
> her prow was fashioned like a swan,
> and light upon her banners laid...

It goes on to describe how the Mariner (father of Elrond Half-Elven and distant ancestor of Aragorn) achieves his mission in the Undying Lands, and being forbidden to set foot again in Middle-earth is sent by the Immortals to journey for ever in a silver, winged ship across the shoreless skies, shining now and forever as the brightest star above Middle-earth, the "star" we know as Venus, herald of the dawn and the evening. An early version of the poem may be found in *The Book of Lost Tales* (Part II), together with an account of its evolution. It began as follows:

> Éarendel arose where the shadow flows
> at Ocean's silent brim;
> through mouth of night as a ray of light
> where the shores are sheer and dim
> he launched his bark like a silver spark
> from the last and lonely sand;
> then on sunlit breath of day's fiery death
> he sailed from Westerland....

If this is close to the heart of Tolkien's poetic vision of the cosmos, it also illustrates the importance of language, of the sound of words, of poetry, for the inner journey that he was engaged in. The "curious thrill" he speaks of is not evoked purely by the sound of the individual words used by Cynewulf, but by their setting in a poetic context, which gives them their musical quality and ability to touch the heart. The phrase in question may be from an explicitly Christian poem, but Tolkien does not immediately jump to an explicitly Christian interpretation (L 297). Nor is he satisfied by the easily available (to him) Germanic and Old Norse references to a star or messenger of this name. These only intrigued him further.

What interests him is primarily the ancient world, the mythic history, evoked by the phrase. He sees this phrase employed by the poet as imbued with a kind of race memory that he wants to spend much of his life recovering, or helping to regenerate. From this fragment, removed from its context in the poem as a whole and combined with other clues and evidence, he senses the possibility of rebuilding the long-lost mythology of pre-Norman England (L 131 and 180).

Language remained the key to this reconstruction, and a glance at the theories of fellow-Inkling Owen Barfield can help us understand how. For Barfield, the development of consciousness, mythology, and language go hand in hand. He believed that human language and consciousness have evolved together from a state of "original participation," in which subject and object, word and thing, were virtually identified, to a state of alienation in which they are separated to such a degree that the sense of connectedness—with nature and with each other—has been lost. The earlier form of consciousness expressed itself primarily in myth, in poetry and metaphor. Ancient language used images of things to express its meaning. Later, with the development of abstract thought, metaphor falls into the background, and for a scientific consciousness detachment and measurement become all-important. This is a necessary stage in the emergence of a new kind of participation, a conscious communion with all things heralded in human evolution (or so Barfield thought, following Steiner) by the appearance of Christ.

The opposite of abstract thought, Barfield tells us, is symbolic thought or imagination. Following Coleridge, he divides *phantasie* into two, on the one hand "fancy" or the mere image-making capacity, and on the other "imagination," which is a creative and perceptive power. (Tolkien prefers to call the higher faculty "Fantasy," so his terminology is reversed, but the basic idea is the same.)

Myth-making or *mythopoeia*, for all the Inklings, is an act of the creative imagination. It is closely related to the poetic roots of language itself. Naming is not merely the attachment of arbitrary labels to things, but involves us in the imaginative/intellectual grasping of *what they are*. To give a name to something is to therefore pick it out from its context, to identify it as a thing-in-itself, and to perceive at least something of its character and purpose in relation to ourselves. Poetry takes this to another level. It discovers the things revealed in experience to be analogies, similes, metaphors, symbols, each in some sense pregnant with inexhaustible meaning. We "know" things more completely by finding the connection between one thing and another, and between myself and all those things, in a way that illuminates both.

The study of etymology, of the origins and evolution of word-forms, could therefore be a journey back in time and consciousness, for the words themselves—and especially the concrete metaphors they were originally based upon—bear traces of original participation. Readers of *The Lord of the Rings* will recall the words of Treebeard to Merry and Pippin: "Real names tell you the story of the things they belong to in my language."

The Notion Club

Some of Tolkien's unfinished stories give us further insights into his attempts to explore the past through language. The "Notion Club Papers" are an example and are especially worth reading because the Notion Club was closely modeled on his experience of the Inklings (though he warns us against identifying them too closely, calling it a "cracked mirror").[4] The second part of the Papers was once labeled "Beyond Lewis, or, Out of the Talkative Planet," and aspects of Tolkien's own self-portrait are evident in the character of Michael George Ramer, the professor of Finno-Ugric philology who is "better known as a writer of romances."

The Papers or "minutes" of the Club (actually written in 1945) were supposed to have been discovered around 2012 and to date from the 1980s. They begin with a discussion of science fiction (including the stories of H. G. Wells, C. S. Lewis, and Olaf Stapledon), and then Ramer leads the Club—and especially Lowdham—into what proves to be a dangerous experiment. Believing that in certain "serious dreams, or visions" we have access to memories and experiences not our own, he claims to have trained himself to "travel" out of his body in this manner. Some of the glimpses he reports are thinly disguised experiences of Tolkien himself, such as the green wave, the tall tower by the sea, and tall, slender trees crowned with blue and gold standing on a green mound (Lothlórien?). Beyond these dreams lay something even more mystical:

> But out of some place beyond the region of dreams, now and again there comes a blessedness, and it soaks through all the levels, and illumines all the scenes through which the mind passes out back into waking, and so it flows out into this life. There it lasts long, but not forever in this world, and memory cannot reach its source. Often we ascribe it to the pictures seen on the margin radiant in its light, as we pass by and out. But a mountain far in the North caught in a slow sunset is not the Sun.

Ramer's journeys take him to alien worlds, far beyond Earth (the "Talkative Planet") and the rest of our solar system, which he experiences as barren of life. Eshúrizel, home of the En-keladim: an inorganic world full of music, resembling a "garden, a paradise of water, metal, stone, like the interwoven variations of vast natural orders of flowers." Minal-Zidar the golden: "absolutely silent and quiescent, a whole small world of one single perfect form, complete, imperishable in Time, finished, at peace, a jewel, a visible word, a realization in material form of contemplation and adoration."

The members of the Club are particularly intrigued by the *names* Ramer comes up with, which he claims belong to his "native language." By this Ramer means what he calls "Old Human, or Primitive Adamic"; that is, the first language of men.

> In language-invention, though you may seem to build only out of material taken from other acquired tongues, it is those elements most near to your native style that you select. In such rare dreams as I was thinking about, far away by oneself in voiceless countries, then your own native language bubbles up, and makes new names for strange new things.

The Elvish En-keladim show Ramer the history of Atlantis in the "Drama of the Silver Tree."

> [They are] sitting round in a circle and singing in that strange, long, long, but never-wearying, uncloying music, endlessly unfolding out of itself, while the song takes visible life among them. The Green Sea flowers in foam, and the Isle rises and opens like a rose in the midst of it. There the Tree opens the starred turf like a silver spear, and grows, and there is a New Light; and the leaves unfold and there is Full Light; and the leaves fall and there is a Rain of Light. Then the Door opens—but no! I have no words for that Fear.

The Club discusses the relationship of myth to history. Jeremy suggests that ancient legends about "the origins of kings, laws, and the fundamental crafts" are not wholly inventions, or at least not mere "fiction": they have more *roots*. "Roots in what?" asks Frankley.

> "In Being, I think I should say," Jeremy answered, "and in human Being; and coming down the scale, in the springs of History and in the designs of Geography—I mean, well, in the pattern of our world as it uniquely is, and of the events in it as seen from a distance. A sort of parallel to the fact that from far away the Earth would be seen as a revolving sunlit globe; and that is a remote truth of enormous effect on us and all we do, though not immediately discernible on earth, where practical men are quite right in regarding the surface as flat and immovable for practical purposes."

Notice how Tolkien turns the tables on the "practical men"—in this case academic historians. Their scientific mentality is being compared here with flat-earthism. He goes on to refine his theory:

> Of course, the pictures presented by the legends may be partly symbolical, they may be arranged in designs that compress, expand, foreshorten, combine, and are not at all realistic or photographic; yet they may tell you something true about the Past.
>
> And mind you, there are also real details, what are called facts, accidents of land-shape and sea-shape, of individual men and their actions, that are caught up: the grains on which the stories crystallize like snowflakes. There was a man called Arthur at the center of the cycle.

Frankley objects that the Arthurian romances are not "real in the same way as true past events are real." Jeremy replies: "I didn't say *in the same way....* There are secondary planes or degrees."

In the Platonic-Romantic tradition of European litera-ture there are many levels of reality. A "Great Chain of Being" stretches from the pure spirits and celestial spheres of imper-ishable crystal down to the changeable realms below the moon. Tolkien is exploring the possible application of this medieval cosmology to time in a way that would reconcile the truths of science with the truths he has discerned in mythol-ogy. In effect, he was doing nothing less than developing a the-ory of myth that would account for his own ongoing, lifelong project, the Silmarillion.

In the story, the Club dwells on the experience of Númenor/ Atlantis. Lowdham is not a "seer" like Ramer, but from the age of ten he has experienced linguistic ghosts that connect him back to the events that Ramer has glimpsed. His real name turns out to be Ælfwine ("elf-friend"), and his father Edwin an explorer who disappeared into the western ocean in a ship called *The Éarendel*. The fact that the final link back to Númenor/Atlantis is provided by a line of fathers and sons is highly significant, for the pattern recurs throughout the Silmarillion. The names Ælf-wine, Errol, Eriol, Alboin, Alwin, Edwin, and Elendil all mean "Elf-friend." Descendants of the first Elendil have the "sea-longing," the haunting desire to travel back to the West.

Together the members of the Club discover that in its last days Númenor—Westernesse, or "the Land of Gift"—was cor-rupted by an evil force called *Zigūr* (called Sauron in *The Lord of the Rings*). Attempting to wrest the secret of immortality from the gods by force, the evil Númenoreans provoke their own destruction. This is when the Papers, too, take a dramatic turn, as the mythic reality the Club is exploring starts to influence the world around them. Their recollection of the downfall of

Númenor overshadowed by the eagles of the true Lords of the West causes a great storm to originate in the Atlantic Ocean, a storm that "slew more men, felled more trees, and cast down more towers, bridges, and other works of Man than a hundred years of wild weather." Rather spookily, since he was writing in 1945, Tolkien places this fictional storm in the year 1987, which was in fact the year of a great storm that many in England and France still remember.

The story is not yet over—Tolkien goes on to connect it with the legends of St. Brendan's Voyage and a journey by Lowdham to Ireland in pursuit of his father—but it was never completed. Interrupted by the need to get the final volume of *The Lord of the Rings* ready for publication, Tolkien never returned to the manuscript, or to the continued development of the Avallonian and Adunaic languages discovered by Lowdham.

We may regret that Tolkien never finished the story, but the Papers had become too chaotic, and in any case they seemed to have fulfilled their purpose by clarifying in his mind the events surrounding the end of Númenor. The energies he would have used in making a publishable story out of the Papers were poured first into the appendices of *The Lord of the Rings*, and then back into the wider waters of the Silmarillion.

It took all the dedication and scholarship of his son Christopher to bring this work into sufficient order to be publishable as *The Silmarillion*, four years after the author's death. But ironically one of the important elements that got lost in the transition was the explicit acknowledgment of the link between father and son in the discovery of the past. The only trace of Ælfwine that remains is Elendil, who now provides a suitably distinguished lineage for Aragorn. Yet Tolkien's filial piety was intense. He once wrote: "The link between father and son is not only of the perishable flesh: it must have something of *aeternitas* about it" (L 45). His own father, Arthur, was taken from him by death when he was only four years old, soon after he and his mother had sailed across the Atlantic Ocean separating England from South Africa. It is not hard to connect Tolkien's longing for the father in the faraway country he could barely remember with the sea-longing expressed in his stories, and to link this with the desire for an ancient world that has been taken away in a time before memory.

This is not an attempt to "explain" the stories, although it may help to account for some of their poignancy. Nevertheless, it gives another level of meaning to a sentence I have quoted in passing: "There was a man called Arthur at the center of the cycle." Tolkien's relationship to his own father became for him a mystical link to the past, to his own past and the past of the race, to the collective unconscious, the roots of the tree of tales. This link between generations, through which life and hope are transmitted from father to son, is also the way back through memory and language from the present world to a world that can be accurately described only in myth.

Tree and Leaf

In the introductory note he wrote for the 1964 edition of *Tree and Leaf* (comprising the famous essay "On Fairy-Stories" and the short story "Leaf by Niggle"), Tolkien mentioned a "great-limbed poplar tree" that had served as his inspiration for his short story.

> It was suddenly lopped and mutilated by its owner, I do not know why. It is cut down now, a less barbarous punishment for any crimes it may have been accused of, such as being large and alive. I do not think it had any friends, or any mourners, except myself and a pair of owls.

This was something more than sentimentality. It was not that he was literally reading human feelings or consciousness into the tree (or the owls!), but that tree was *present* and *alive* to him in a way it is not to most other people. Tolkien saw natural things freighted with the depth of meaning that all things possess, being rooted in the mind of God. God does not create things simply to fill up space. God creates for a reason, and the ultimate reason for his creation is love. Each thing, and especially each living thing, is a word, a symbol, a revelation. Each is a note, or a theme, in some great music. At any rate, it is more than itself: that is, more than the thing most people see when they look at it.

The symbolic properties of the tree have been obvious to many people and cultures. Jewish and Christian Scriptures place a tree or trees at the center of Paradise. The Norse legends that Tolkien loved speak of the World Tree *Yggdrasil,* whose trunk runs through the heart of Middle-earth. Yggdrasil is a great ash, whose branches support the Nine Worlds and reach to the heavens above Asgard. Its roots reach down to Hel, at its foot is a fountain of wisdom, and upon it the father-god Odin (Woden) hung wounded for nine days and nights before achieving a knowledge of the Mysteries and his own resurrection. "Middle-earth " (Midgard) gets its name, obviously, from its position between heaven and hell.

The tree of tales, similarly, links all the worlds and is the source of wisdom for those who hang upon it. The way a tree grows—slowly, incrementally, organically—is the way myths and legends grow, the way a tradition grows. It is the way Tolkien's *legendarium* grew. There may be sudden spurts of growth in good weather, boughs may be lopped off or felled by a storm, there may be seasons when the tree wears green, or bursts forth in flower or fruit, but at all times there is a sap and a spirit that runs through it and makes it a living thing. It is more than the soil and minerals, the sunlight and water that compose it. In one Oxford churchyard there stands a tree that was young at the time of King Arthur, and may survive until his return. For fifteen hundred years it has dwelt there, maybe the oldest living thing in Oxford.

In "Leaf by Niggle" Tolkien uses the metaphor of the tree in a way that affords us a rare glimpse into the way he understood his own art and its importance for his life. The story is a kind of extended parable or allegory. Tolkien tells us in his introductory note that he woke up one morning with the whole story clear in his mind, and wrote it in haste. This was around 1939, when he was beginning to despair of ever finding out what had become of Gandalf or who Strider was. The hobbits had arrived at Bree: it was uncertain whether he would ever get them farther. The carping of his academic colleagues, critical of him for wasting his energy on fairy-tales, and the demands of academic life, not to mention his family, must have been keenly felt. And war was looming.

The story concerns an amateur painter called Niggle, neighbor to a man called Parish. Niggle is working on a great painting: a huge tree set against a mountainous landscape. It began, Tolkien says, with an attempt to paint a single leaf caught in the wind. Niggle, of course, represents the author: his name reveals the earthly, day-to-day nature of artistic work. The "leaf in the wind" might be the fragment of Anglo-Saxon poetry that we have already encountered. Tolkien must often have felt that his whole life was being frittered away on small textual details when the whole vista of the Silmarillion, for so long looming ever vaster in his mind, remained to be expressed. (Readers of *The History of Middle-Earth* will be well aware just how much niggling Tolkien actually did!)

Mr. Parish next door, of course, represents all those people who make demands on the artist's time and take him away from what he feels he *ought* to be doing. As a Christian, Tolkien viewed every such person as a representative of Christ, a member of Christ's "flock," and accepted the responsibility laid upon him by the Gospel to "love your neighbor as yourself." But most of Parish's demands appear at the time to be trivial, not least the exaggerated claim to illness that leads to Niggle himself catching cold and dying before his work is nearly completed.

Tolkien is presenting a humorous self-portrait here, and one that we can all identify with to some extent. Many of us have delusions of self-importance and by contrast view the needs of others as less weighty than our own, regarding at times even the common courtesies of small talk and social chit-chat as a tedious burden. The artist, driven and on fire with his inspiration, is liable to be even worse in this respect than most.

Much of the story is a description, in allegorical terms, of the after-death state known as Purgatory. Since this Catholic doctrine became something of a bone of contention during the Reformation, it is worth remarking that Tolkien's picture of it here is quite sensible and appealing. In fact it is clearly a kind of healing process. Exactly how long it takes is mysterious, since after death the normal measures of time are not applicable. It might well be said to take place in the very moment of dying. Tolkien describes Niggle as being placed in the "Workhouse" for a century or so—clearly a bit of a joke against the popular notion of "time in Purgatory," which as a well-informed Catholic he must have known to be false. Nor is the point of the Workhouse to punish Niggle, but rather to teach him to do "one thing at a time" until he feels "quieter inside."

There follows an examination of his conscience by the Holy Trinity (three mysterious Voices overheard in the dark). Niggle's fundamental good will, despite all the imperfections of his bad temper and grudging, resentful attitude, is what finally counts in his favor. In Catholic teaching, Purgatory is the state of those who have been judged worthy of Heaven, but "only as through fire" (1 Cor. 3:15). The judgment of the soul has already taken place, though in the story Niggle is ready to overhear the judgment only when his purification is virtually complete.

Now that his perception of the world has been washed clean, he is able to see all things as coming straight from the hands of God, as a "gift." He is sent off into the sunlight on a special train, arriving in an unexpected place: the very landscape he had been trying to paint. The Tree has been perfected, for it turns out the important thing on earth was not the accomplishment of the artist, which is always doomed to frustration, but the *intention*, which will be fulfilled in Heaven. Furthermore the best parts of the Tree were not those which he had painted without interruption, but those in which his relationship to his neighbor Mr. Parish had played a part.

Chapter Two

The Hobbit:
There and Back Again

The magic word "Hobbit" emerged spontaneously in an idle moment at the beginning of the 1930s, while Tolkien was marking some student essays and came across a blank page. "In a hole in the ground there lived a hobbit," he doodled—and then began to wonder what the word meant.

One might have speculated that the word unconsciously came by merging the word "rabbit" with the word "hob" (an old English name for a household elf or sprite), except that Tolkien always denied rabbits had anything to do with it. On further investigation, Hobbits turned out to be between two and four feet tall when fully grown (although they used to be taller), a "merry folk" who dressed in bright colors and seldom wore shoes because their feet "had tough leathery soles and were clad in thick curling hair." Little interested in machinery more complicated than a water mill (though they possessed clocks, umbrellas, and fireworks), they were a settled, unadventurous, agrarian people, an affectionate caricature of the rural English whom Tolkien knew as a child in and around the village of Sarehole, which he once in an interview described as "a kind of lost paradise."

Most of the best children's stories were composed with real children in mind, and Tolkien's *The Hobbit or There and Back Again*, to give it its full title, is no exception. By 1930 Tolkien's own children were thirteen (John), ten (Michael), six (Christopher), and one (Priscilla). The story was initially written for them and completed in first draft by 1932. During the subsequent years, Tolkien lent the story to C. S. Lewis and also to various friends and acquaintances, whose positive reactions led to its being submitted to the publisher Stanley Unwin. It was accepted on the strength of a positive review by Stanley Unwin's then ten-year-old son, Rayner, in 1936. The first edition is dated 1937.

The hobbit of the title, Bilbo Baggins, is plucked from his sedate and rather luxurious existence at Bag End in Hobbiton by the mysterious wizard Gandalf. Gandalf appears before his round, green door when Bilbo is around fifty years old (young for a hobbit) and arranges for him to accompany the distinguished dwarf Thorin Oakenshield and his twelve companions in a quest to regain lost treasure from a dragon called Smaug. (Bilbo is chosen partly to avoid bad luck by making the number up to fourteen.) What begins as a comedy gradually becomes more serious, as Bilbo discovers his courage, acquires a magic ring under the Misty Mountains, and saves the dwarves from various perils in the course of the long and hazardous journey, finally becoming, if not a dragon-slayer as Tolkien originally intended (though he discovers the dragon's vulnerable spot) then at least a burglar of the dragon's lair and eventually an effective diplomat. In the Battle of Five Armies, representing goblins (orcs) and wolves, men, elves, and dwarves, not to mention eagles, Bilbo is caught up in the great events of Middle-earth.

The story, like the "Father Christmas Letters" that Tolkien liked to write and illustrate for his children each year (and that were eventually published in 1976 and 2004), was not originally planned or conceived as part of the mythology he had begun writing in 1914, although he soon began to think of ways of revising it to fit into the grand narrative of the Third Age of Middle-earth that had begun to emerge. (The first volume of *The Lord of the Rings* appeared in 1954, following the revised second edition of *The Hobbit* in 1951.) In what follows I will be commenting on the final rather than the intermediate versions, and page references will be to the edition listed in my Bibliography. For those who are interested, a detailed scholarly study by John D. Rateliff, *The History of the Hobbit*, traces in detail the evolution of the text through numerous rewritings and includes fascinating commentaries on the main characters and events.

The Journey Home

G. K. Chesterton begins his book *Orthodoxy* by describing a hypothetical "romance" about a man who sets sail from England in order to discover a new country. By chance he ends up returning to England, thinking it is the new place, and finds himself looking at familiar things as if for the first time. Chesterton asks: "How can we contrive to be at once astonished at the world and yet at home in it?" It is a recurrent question in his writing. Similarly, Marcel Proust remarks: "The only real voyage of discovery consists not in seeking new landscapes but in having new eyes" (Marcel Proust).

The Hobbit and later *The Lord of the Rings* both describe such a voyage of discovery. Each novel describes a journey from the Shire and back, with the Hobbits (or in the case of the first book, just Bilbo) returning so changed by their experiences that they see and act very differently. They have "grown."

Bilbo's chance acquisition of the magic ring under the Misty Mountains—a ring that makes the wearer invisible (its other properties, and dangers, are not yet apparent)—corresponds to a growth in his own inner confidence, as he learns

independence of mind and begins to use his own gifts and talents. (C. G. Jung would have called it "individuation.") Dangerous adventures alternating with moments of respite—usually
involving large quantities of food—provide him with a series
of initiations. The journey begins and ends at Bag End, and in
both cases with an unexpected tea party. But (as Jane Chance
has pointed out) Bilbo's attitude to his guests has been changed
by the intervening adventure, marking his growth from selfish
squire to generous host, welcoming his guests with joy, and in
his final words "thanking goodness" for being, as Gandalf says,
"quite a little fellow in a wide world after all."

Bilbo is a hero virtually inconceivable in an earlier era
(except as comic relief, perhaps), able to assume a central role
in the narrative despite his relatively peripheral role in the
great events of dragon-slaying and battle. Tolkien renders the
heroic motives of Thorin and the others all too transparent,
and we see the pride and selfishness that lies behind them as
the dwarf reclaims his kingdom and refuses to share his new-
found wealth with those of other races who brought about the
victory. Yet through Bilbo's friendship with him we are led to
see deeper still, to the goodness that lies beneath and that
emerges in the form of repentance as Thorin lies on his death-
bed. Not only is Bilbo himself transformed by his adventures,
but he also becomes a transformative influence on others, a
catalyst for spiritual growth.

Of Dragons

"I desired dragons with a profound desire," wrote Tolkien of
his younger self in "On Fairy-Stories." In fact, Humphrey Carpenter's biography of Tolkien informs us that he began to
compose his own first story about them at the age of seven.
His mother pointed out that he could not say "a green great

dragon," but only "a great green dragon"; thus possibly divert-ing his attention from dragons to language and philology. But dragons remained a fascination—particularly Sigurd's dragon Fafnir and the dragon who becomes Beowulf's nemesis—and they re-emerged in force for the destruction of Gondolin in one of his earliest mythological stories. (The Green Dragon reappears in *The Fellowship of the Ring* as the name of a pub in Bywater frequented by Sam Gamgee and Ted Sandyman.)

Why were dragons so significant in his imaginative life? The reason, he tells us, is that the dragon is a creature entirely of Faërie, of the Other-world, and it is this world, or a glimpse of it, that he desired. Not "in the neighborhood," of course, where a real-life dragon would be much too alarming, but "over the hills and far away," where the heart may venture though the body quails. (Tolkien's complex and beautiful short story, *Smith of Wootton Major*, though not a dragon tale, is all about this longing for Faërie.)

Bilbo has fond memories of Gandalf's tales at parties "about dragons and goblins and giants and the rescue of prin-cesses and the unexpected luck of widows' sons" (p. 13). In other words, he is in a position similar to most of us; he is a lover of tales, an armchair-traveler. Unfortunately for him, it turns out that the Other-world is not so far away after all: the Shire is just one little neglected corner of a "wide world" in which such adventures truly happen. (The implication being, of course, that to the extent that we are encouraged to identify with Bilbo, the same may be true of us.)

And at the climax of the adventure into which he is pre-cipitated by the wizard is the magnificent red-gold dragon Smaug, perhaps the last of his race—at least in that part of the world. The goal of the expedition is to recover the treasure of Thror, the King Under the Mountain (Thorin's grandfather);

a treasure over which Smaug now gloats and sleeps. The vast hoard itself, when Bilbo finally sees it, does more than take his breath away:

> There are no words left to express his staggerment, since Men changed the language that they learned of elves in the days when all the world was wonderful. Bilbo had heard tell and sing of dragon-hoards before, but the splendor, the lust, the glory of such treasure had never come home to him. His heart was filled and pierced with enchantment and with the desire of dwarves; and he gazed motionless, almost forgetting the frightful guardian, at the gold beyond price and count. (pp. 184–85)

Notice how, even in a seemingly offhand remark, Tolkien makes what, in the light of his wider mythology, is actually a profound observation about the nature of language. He implies not only that the Elves were the inventors and teachers of language, but that the first languages were richer and more eloquent than ours—more capable of expressing a response to wonder. The very function of Faërie, and of "fairy-tales," is to awaken that sense of wonder, that awareness of a world enchanted and glorious that we have lost along with our sense of poetry and awe. On arriving at the Dragon, we have arrived, with Bilbo, at the heart of Faërie.

The account of Bilbo's encounter with Smaug, who is one of the most vivid characterizations of a dragon in all literature, is modeled on Beowulf's encounter with the dragon at the end of Tolkien's favorite epic poem. Like the nameless thief in *Beowulf*, Bilbo stirs the dragon's wrath by stealing a golden cup from under his nose, with similar results. As he says to the angry dwarves, who accuse him of rousing the dragon prematurely by stealing from the hoard: "I was not engaged to kill dragons, that is warrior's work, but to steal treasure" (p. 188).

Bilbo is no warrior. In Gandalf's words, he is a "chosen and selected burglar" (p. 27)—a thief, in other words. This puts him in good company, strange as it may seem. Folklore is full of tricksters and thieves, from Ali Baba, Loki, and Jack the Giant-Killer to Jason, stealer of the Golden Fleece from another dragon. In most of these stories, the thievery is part of a larger story of restoration, of the recovery of what had been lost, or what rightfully belonged elsewhere. Bilbo's story is of this type, with the further linguistic twist that the word "burglar" sounds delightfully domestic and banal in contrast to the heroic tale in which it is set: once again Tolkien is using language itself to weave our ordinary world, the world of the daily newspaper over the morning coffee, into an epic romance.

The Arkenstone

The "burglar" in Bilbo finally comes into his own when he steals from Smaug's hoard the one treasure that Thorin values above all others: the Arkenstone. Here we are dealing with another profound archetype. The theme of "holy gems" full of mysterious light runs all the way through Tolkien's writing, from the three Silmarils made by the great Elven craftsman Fëanor to the seven Palantíri, the Phial of Galadriel, the Elessar or green stone worn by Aragorn, the white gem "like a star" that Arwen gives to Frodo (to help him when the "memory of the fear and the darkness" troubles him), and the Three Rings that assist the Wise in their long war with Sauron—Nenya, Narya, and Vilya—each bearing a gem of a different color (white, red, and blue, representing water, fire, and air respectively).

In her book *Splintered Light* Verlyn Flieger shows that Tolkien's writing is very much about the history and adventures of light (and thus manifestations of the "Word," which is according to the opening of the Gospel of John "the light of men"), beginning with great Lamps that Aulë created to illuminate the world in its first design, and later the golden and silver light of the Two Trees that illuminated Valinor after the destruction of the Lamps. The Sun and Moon that we know preserve the faint radiance of the last flower and fruit of the dying Trees, after they were poisoned by Morgoth and Ungoliant (the ancestor of Shelob).

In Tolkien's writing one loses count of the number of times he refers to a "light" in the eyes of his characters—even Gollum (a "fell" light, a "green" light, a "pale" light, and so on). A common image, too, is that of the "light on the brow," sometimes shining from a jewel worn there and sometimes simply present, as in the case of Aragorn in Frodo's vision of him. The mythical background to this is the fact that light represents consciousness, and the quality of the light either the quality of that consciousness, or of the essence of the person.

The light on the brow, of course, is familiar to us as the "third eye" of the sage, the "single" eye of which Jesus speaks when giving his disciples instructions on how to pray the Lord's Prayer in the Gospel of Matthew. "The eye is the lamp of the body," he says. "So, if your eye is sound [and the word also means 'single'], your whole body will be full of light; but if your eye is not sound, your whole body will be full of darkness" (Matt. 6:22–23). (The single fiery Eye of Sauron is the demonic counterpart of this third eye.) In Tolkien's 1967 story *Smith of Wootton Major*, the "single eye" is represented by a magic star that is baked into a Great Cake every twenty-four years, always finding its way into the slice of a worthy child. Thereafter it shines on his brow as a passport to the Land of Faëry itself.

Ultimately all awareness comes from God, and all things are seen most truly as they are in the light of the divine vision, which creates even as it knows (hence the first words of God in the

Christian and Hebrew Bible, when the world is created: "Let there be light"). But mythical jewels, or other objects containing light, mediate and represent an aspect of this awareness. Thus when a holy jewel such as a Silmaril is worn, whether on the brow or (in the case of the Nauglamír of the Dwarves) in the setting of a necklace, not only does it shine and surround the wearer with light, but it makes the self of the wearer appear beautiful—as if one could see them with the eyes of love.

In early drafts of *The Hobbit*, the word "Arkenstone" served as a synonym for "Silmaril," indicating a profound link to the greater *legendarium* in Tolkien's imagination. The Arkenstone as it later appeared in the final redaction was, of course, a lesser stone than those that contained the blended light of the Two Trees and that ended, we are told in *The Silmarillion*, "one in the airs of heaven, and one in the fires of the heart of the world, and one in the deep waters." Nevertheless, it is of a similar nature, a vessel hallowed for containing light—and here the associations of the word "Ark" become particularly significant. (There is a Jewish legend that God created a gem containing the original light of creation, that was passed via Adam and his righteous descendants to Noah, who used it to illuminate the Ark; but this may be coincidental.)

In view of the fact that the light in the Arkenstone is symbolically linked to the light of divine vision, the vision of love, it is not surprising that it becomes a temptation and a danger to those who lust after it. Tolkien's background mythology makes it very clear that Evil lusts after the Good that it cannot possess or truly understand, and will clasp that Beauty to itself even though it can experience the light only as fire and torment.

> "The Arkenstone! The Arkenstone!" murmured Thorin in the dark, half dreaming with his chin upon his knees. "It was like a globe with a thousand faces; it shone like silver in the

firelight, like water in the sun, like snow under the stars, like rain upon the Moon!" (p. 197)

"The Eagles Are Coming!"

Like dragons and holy gems and magic rings, not to mention spiders and wolves, eagles are a common motif in Tolkien's writing. In *The Lord of the Rings* they will rescue Gandalf from Saruman and the Ringbearers from the fires of Mount Doom. In *The Hobbit* they rescue Gandalf, Bilbo, and the dwarves from burning trees set aflame by the goblins waiting below, and they play a crucial role in the Battle of Five Armies. (Bilbo's cry, "The eagles are coming!" is consciously echoed by Pippin just before he, too, loses consciousness on the field of battle before the Black Gate in *The Return of the King*.) In his amusing letter to Forrest J. Ackerman in 1958, containing his critique of a proposed film treatment of *The Lord of Rings*, Tolkien had to warn against the overuse of this device (L 210).

The importance of the eagles derives in Tolkien's mythology from their association with Manwë, the king of the "gods" (Valar) and husband of Elbereth/Varda, the Queen of Heaven. In *The Silmarillion* we are told that this "highest and holiest of the Valar" set his throne upon the pinnacle of Taniquetil, a mountain that stood on the borders of the sea facing toward Middle-earth. "Spirits in the shapes of hawks and eagles flew ever to and fro from his halls; and their eyes could see to the depths of the sea, and pierce the hidden caverns beneath the world." Spirits (Maiar) clothed in the bodies of eagles, then, were the messengers and emissaries of Manwë, just as the great wargs and werewolves were evil spirits given bodies of service to the great Enemy. In writing about the fall of Númenor in *The Silmarillion*, Tolkien describes the thunderclouds in the form of eagles that signal the anger of the Lords of West against the men who aspire to immortality.

The eagle is associated in mythology both with Odin and with Zeus. It is an eagle of Zeus (perhaps Zeus himself), carrying the child Ganymede the Trojan to be the god's cup-bearer, which is depicted on the Inklings' favorite pub-sign at the Eagle and Child in Oxford. It is impossible that the image was not associated in some way with the eagles in Tolkien's mythology, especially with the scene in which Bilbo is borne by an eagle to its eyrie in the Misty Mountains. Bilbo's adventure is comic rather than epic, since he escapes the burning tree only by clinging to Dori's ankles, but on entering the eagle's world he is touching something very deep in Tolkien's unconscious mind. As messengers of the gods, the Eagles stand at the border between waking awareness and the darkness of sleep, with all the potentiality for transformation that implies. It is appropriate that Bilbo, like Pippin later, sees them just before he enters the realm of unconsciousness. The arrival of the eagles is like a mini-*eucatastrophe*, a touch of grace, a turning point that changes everything, bringing hope where there had been none.

The Transformation of Bilbo

The key stylistic innovation that appears in this book and became the foundation for *The Lord of the Rings* reflects a fundamental tension in Tolkien's imagination. On the one hand he was writing this story for his own children. On the other, the mythology, the Silmarillion that had begun to take shape in his notebooks since the war, was pulling the narrative toward a very different genre of writing: archaic, poetic, high-flown, epic. The result was what C. S. Lewis describes as a "shift in tone" within *The Hobbit* itself, a change in the style of the language sufficient to carry the reader almost without realizing it from the everyday world a modern child can identify with (a world of tea time, umbrellas, and pocket handkerchiefs) into the universe of mythology, high romance, and chivalry—and back again.

It makes sense that the shift comes about after the encounter with the dragon, for dragons often symbolize a great spiritual and moral challenge. That is why they so often feature in Quest stories. They are usually defeated by a hero acting alone. Their serpentine shape connects them with the Serpent in Eden's garden, who is struck down to crawl upon the earth as a divine punishment for tempting the woman and her husband. The magical influence of the dragon's voice also harks back to Eden, as does the association with pride, greed, and possessiveness, even to the extent of infecting the hoard with the power to stir greed in others, for the sin of our first ancestors was to steal a treasure that was forbidden to them. Thus in the combat with a dragon, the hero is doing nothing less than attempting to vanquish the root of his own weakness and tendency to sin.

Bilbo's combat with the dragon Smaug is not with weapons and violence, but with words—a verbal sparring match that some people find the most entertaining scene in the book. Smaug has (as the author remarks) "rather an overwhelming personality"—certainly when compared to the cowardly dragon Chrysophlax in Tolkien's 1949 dragon-slaying tale *Farmer Giles of Ham*—while Bilbo's confidence and cleverness in making riddles has grown enormously since his game with Gollum under the Misty Mountains. His adventures in Mirkwood—notably rescuing the dwarves from the evil spiders and the wood elves—had already begun to change him. "He felt a different person, and much fiercer and bolder in spite of an empty stomach, as he wiped his sword on the grass and put it back in its sheath" (not before giving it the name "Sting"). The final interior battle is won just before Bilbo actually sees the dragon, as he hesitates at the end of the tunnel leading to Smaug's lair. "Going on from there was the bravest thing he ever did. The tremendous things that happened afterwards were as nothing compared to it. He fought the real battle in the tunnel alone, before he ever saw the vast danger that lay in wait" (p. 184).

Eventually, by appealing to the dragon's absurd pride, Bilbo manages to persuade him to reveal his one weakness—the bare patch in his diamond waistcoat that will later be the target of Bard's fatal arrow. Bilbo escapes singed but alive (transformation often enough takes place through fire), and the reader does not find it odd that he now has the self-confidence to appropriate the Arkenstone, or to try to use it as a bargaining chip in the negotiations between Thorin's dwarves and the armies of Esgaroth and the Forest, who are camped before the Mountain.

The shift in tone from humdrum and comic to high epic is reflected in the voice of the narrator, who at the beginning of the book is telling us, "He had a horrible thought that the cakes might run short, and then he—as the host: he knew his duty and stuck to it however painful—he might have to go without," by the end of the story, after the death of the dragon, is saying such things as: "Many took ill of wet and cold and sorrow that night, and afterwards died, who had escaped uninjured from the ruin of the town; and in the days that followed there was much sickness and great hunger." The tone adopted by the narrator—by turns patronizing, pompous, and cruel—is one of the interesting features of the book. In *Tolkien's Art* (a book about Tolkien's multi-layered craftsmanship) Jane Chance argues that the persona of the narrator is a deliberate literary construction by the author, intended as a satire on the literary critics he despised. Tolkien grew to regard it as a lapse in judgment, and in 1960 he considered rewriting the entire book in the more detached, "mature" style of *The Lord of the Rings*.

In the face of all this stylistic complexity, Bilbo's speech patterns remain constant. "Really you know, things are impossible. Personally I am tired of the whole affair. I wish I was back in the West in my own home, where folk are more reasonable." Constant, that is, until the death of Thorin, where the two worlds truly come together in what is a scene of reconciliation on many levels:

> "Farewell, King under the Mountain! This is a bitter adventure, if it must end so; and not a mountain of gold can amend it. Yet I am glad that I have shared in your perils—that has been more than any Baggins deserves."

In the end it is Gandalf who sums it up. "My dear Bilbo! Something is the matter with you! You are not the hobbit that you were." His relatives back home agree: the Sackville-Bagginses "never admitted that the returned Baggins was genuine." The reader knows that he has been named "elf-Friend" by the King of the Wood Elves—a title of some resonance in Tolkien's literary universe (equivalent to Ælfwine and Elendil). He now lives between the two worlds, the everyday domestic world of his fellow hobbits, and the world of dwarves, elves, and wizards. Some years after his return to Bag End, Balin and Gandalf drop by for tea, and the book ends with a speech from Gandalf that ties Bilbo's story into the tapestry of events that Providence is weaving through history—the "great story" of which we are all a part.

To Bilbo's comment that "the prophecies of the old songs have turned out to be true, after a fashion," since with the dragon's death the river "runs with gold," Gandalf replies, "Of course! And why should not they prove true? Surely you don't disbelieve the prophecies, because you had a hand in bringing them about yourself? You don't really suppose, do you, that all your adventures and escapes were managed by mere luck, just for your sole benefit?"

Chapter Three

A Very Great Story

Well, there you are: a hobbit amongst the Urukhai. Keep up your hobbitry in heart, and think that all stories feel like that when you are in them. You are inside a very great story!

— J. R. R. Tolkien to his son Christopher
during the Second World War (L 66)

Twenty thousand Allied soldiers died on the first day of fighting in the Battle of the Somme. To prevent his feelings from "festering," Tolkien says he began to write:

> in grimy canteens, at lectures in cold fogs, in huts full of blasphemy and smut, or by candle light in bell-tents, even some down in dugouts under shell fire. It did not make for efficiency and present-mindedness, of course, and I was not a good officer.... (L 66)

The Lancashire Fusiliers won a record number of Victoria Crosses for acts of bravery in that campaign. Tolkien won no medals, but he had come to know and respect the heroes of the first "modern" war: ordinary Tommies who fought and died in the mud with all the indomitable humor and dogged courage of Hobbits. "My 'Sam Gamgee' is indeed a reflection of the English soldier," he wrote, "of the privates and batmen I knew in the 1914 war, and recognized as so far superior to myself."[5] *The Lord of the Rings* was an exploration of English heroism in the wars that laid the foundations of the modern world.

The Lord of the Rings

The Hobbit was an unexpected success, and Tolkien's publishers wanted a sequel. Of course, what he wanted to offer them was the Silmarillion, but they demanded "more hobbits," and this meant that he had to start again with the little people: Bilbo, Frodo, Sam, Merry, and Pippin. Thus providentially what we end up with in the new book is not a chronicle of mythological wars, but another journey "there and back again" from the mundane to the epic, the everyday to the heroic and back to the mundane. Even more than in the shorter book, this was a literary bridge that proved effective in carrying traffic in both directions. It transposes the hobbits into an epic universe, and through them it brings the epic qualities of nobility and courage into the world of the Shire.

In developing his sequel, Tolkien reworked the first version of *The Hobbit* to make it more clearly an episode in the wider history of Middle-earth, a branch on the tree of his Silmarillion. The finding of the Ring under the Misty Mountains became now the center of the story, from having been an "accident along the way." It is revealed as something long sought by the Enemy: the One Ring cut from his hand at the end of the Second Age and now needed to restore his full power. Bilbo's earlier account of the finding of the Ring, in which Gollum had freely given him the Ring as a prize for winning the riddle competition—an account that had been revised in later editions of *The Hobbit*—was explained in the Prologue of the longer work as evidence that the Ring itself had begun quickly to work on his mind and heart, as it had long before upon Gollum, being inhabited by a part of its Master's evil spirit. The new book was therefore painted on a much vaster canvas, with a much greater range of colors, many of them unexpectedly dark and some piercingly bright.

The new story employed the same simple structure as *The Hobbit* to provide the backbone of the plot: a journey into the wild, consisting of a series of light and dark moments, brushes with death alternating with respite in the "homely houses" of Butterbur, Bombadil, Elrond, Galadriel, and Faramir. The goal of the quest is not to retrieve a treasure but to lose one: the Ring must be "unmade" in the fire of its forging, cast into Mount Doom under the very eye of the Dark Lord. If it fails and the Ring returns to its maker, his power to rule will be vastly increased. Elves and Men once successfully opposed him, but an age has passed and the free peoples have become depleted and divided. The existence of the Ring, even outside Sauron's possession, poses the main threat; whereas if it is destroyed, the link binding the Dark Lord's armies and even his own physical substance will be dissolved. Bilbo's heir, Frodo, volunteers to carry the Ring to Mordor:

> An overwhelming longing to rest and remain at peace by Bilbo's side in Rivendell filled all his heart. At last with an effort he spoke, and wondered to hear his own words, as if some other will was using his small voice.
>
> "I will take the Ring," he said, "though I do not know the way."

(It may *feel* like another's will, but that it is truly his own is implied by the fact that he speaks with an effort, against the pressure of a selfish desire. Yet Tolkien's "as if" does carry some weight: in key passages this phrase usually means more than it says. There is another will involved here, but it is a will that does not force or dominate, a will that strengthens our own when we try to do the right thing.)

Frodo is supported along the way by a fellowship of eight companions chosen in Rivendell. The Hobbits are represented by Sam, Merry, and Pippin. Men are represented by Boromir and the ranger Aragorn, the latter now revealed as the heir to the long-vacant throne of Gondor. Legolas for the Elves, Gimli for the Dwarves, and Gandalf complete the Nine. Tolkien gives each of these major protagonists a story of his own, interwoven with the others in a complicated, almost musical harmony that converges on a double climax (one at Mount Doom, and one in the Shire) as the quest is achieved. There is a tenth strand, too, which pulls the whole together, and it is the story of Gollum, the Ring's previous owner (or victim), who pursues it to the very end.

Quite why the Ring cannot simply be transported to Mount Doom by friendly eagles is never explained, but it is strongly implied that the task is one that can be achieved only in this, the hard way. The Ring is a spiritual force that must be carried by the weakest and humblest of creatures, and one to whom the task has been "appointed" (by Providence). Naturally, the plan appears as nothing less than folly to the worldly wise, and this is precisely the reason it is finally adopted. As Gandalf says, "Let folly be our cloak, a veil before the eyes of the Enemy! For he is very wise, and weighs all things to a nicety in the scales of his malice." The Enemy cannot suspect that those who hold the Ring will refuse to use it, and even seek to destroy it.

Already the Christian ethos of the book has become apparent:

> For God's foolishness is wiser than human wisdom, and God's weakness is stronger than human strength.... God chose what is foolish in the world to shame the wise; God chose what is weak in the world to shame the strong; God chose what is low and despised in the world, things that are not, to reduce to nothing things that are. (1 Cor. 1:25–28)

In fact, as the adventure proceeds, Frodo emerges as a very "Christian" type of hero. For Christians the true hero is not the one who succeeds in imposing his own will on others by virtue of outward, physical strength, or even by the inner strength that comes from intelligence and moderation of appetite. He allows himself to be humiliated and crucified. He refuses earthly respect and glory for the sake of something much greater: not merely his own integrity, but the will of the Father in heaven; not for the self, in other words, but for the transcendent Other, for God, and for neighbor. In Frodo's case, he does what he knows he must for the sake of others: "I tried to save the Shire, and it has been saved, but not for me."

Christianity does not simply deny the traditional heroic virtues, but transforms them, raising them to a higher level. Saint Paul is therefore able to emphasize the heroic qualities of Christ almost as though he were describing a traditional military chieftain (Col. 1:20; 2:15). But what is defeated by this hero, what is wrestled to the ground and destroyed, is nothing less than death itself.

Furthermore, for Christianity, since every person is equally important in the eyes of God, *anyone and everyone* can be a hero. You do not have to be a member of the elite, or the warrior caste, nor just a representative of the people. The poor are raised up to the thrones of princes, the strong are humbled, and the rich are sent empty away. As Elrond says: "This is the hour of the Shire-folk, when they arise from their quiet fields to shake the towers and counsels of the Great."

The day Frodo and his companions set out on their mission in the depths of winter is given by Tolkien in the narrative as December 25. The date serves Tolkien well, for it was a Pagan festival long before it became a Christian one, but at the same time it signals to the Christian reader the fact that there is a connection between the mission of the Ring-bearer and that of Christ, who was sent out not from Rivendell but from his mother's womb on the same date.[6]

The mission of Frodo increasingly resembles that of Christ as the journey approaches its end. The slow passage of the Dead Marshes, surrounded by the faint lights and uncanny faces of the dead warriors, and of Shelob's Lair on the borders of Mordor where he falls to the ground, both recall the Garden of Gethsemane, not least because Frodo is betrayed to Shelob under cover of darkness by the companion he tried to save (Gollum). The long carrying of the Ring to Mount Doom, as it grows in weight and power, dragging him to the ground, resembles the way of the cross. The help that Sam gives him in bearing the burden reminds us of the man called Simeon, dragooned by the soldiers into helping Jesus with his cross when it became too heavy for him.

The apocalyptic events that ensue are narrated in a way that inevitably recalls the Book of Revelation, from the rescue of Frodo and Sam from the slopes of the wrecked mountain by eagles (Rev. 12:14) to the token of Frodo's eventual transformation, the "white gem like a star" he is given by Arwen when she offers him her place on the ship to the West. "To everyone who conquers I will give some of the hidden manna, and I will give a white stone, and on the white stone is written a new name which no one knows except the one who receives it" (Rev. 2:17). The triumphant song of the eagle, "Sing and be glad, all ye children of the West, for your king shall come again," reminds us in mood and tone of the words of the seventh angel of the Apocalypse, "The kingdom of the world has become the kingdom of our Lord and of his Messiah, and he will reign forever and ever" (Rev. 11:15).

The Triumph of Mercy

In all these ways, and in the persistent motif of death and resurrection, Tolkien's Christian genius reveals itself. Nowhere is the subtlety of this genius more visible than in a final twist of the plot within the inner chamber of Mount Doom itself. This deserves some closer attention, for it marks an important difference between Frodo and Christ. Frodo is no mere allegorical stand-in, but a rounded character in his own right. On the very brink of success, his free will having taken him as far as it can, he renounces the quest and claims the Ring for his own. It becomes clear that his ability to cast it away has been eroded by the task of bearing it so far. His assertion of ownership over the Ring signifies the loss of his self-possession, and the words he uses betray this: he says, "I do not choose now to do what I came to do. I will not do this deed. The Ring is mine."

Note that he does not say, "I choose...I do," but rather "I do not choose...I will not do." Behind this choice of words lies a great weight of tradition—indeed, a whole theory of ethics. The Christian reader may discern an echo of St. Paul's words: "I can will what is right, but I cannot do it" (Rom. 7:18–19). What is being suggested is that ethics, or right behavior, hinges on *what we have the power to do*. Frodo sees himself as choosing—choosing to claim the Ring. But in fact he has lost the power not to claim it. Christian ethics is about attaining freedom, which does not mean the freedom to do whatever we want but rather the *power to do the right thing*.

Tolkien wrote of Frodo's failure that it reflected the fact that the power of Evil in the world cannot, in the end, be defeated by us on our own, however "good" we may try to be (L 191). By implicitly denying the heresy of Pelagianism (the idea that we can become good entirely by our own power), Tolkien is simply being realistic about our situation in a fallen world. This is not pessimism, however; for while we cannot save ourselves, *we can yet be saved*.

A reader quotes St. Paul's remark (1 Cor. 10:13) that God "will not let you be tested beyond your strength, but with the testing he will also provide the way out so that you may be able to endure it," but Tolkien responds to this by evoking the cases, so familiar in the modern world, of prisoners issuing from captivity broken and insane, perhaps brainwashed by their captors, where no such immediate deliverance by God was available. Such people should be judged by their original intentions, not by their moral "failure" under intolerable torment. In relation to Frodo, he writes (in L 191) that a more appropriate Bible passage would be those familiar lines from the Lord's Prayer: "Lead us not into temptation, but deliver us from evil."

For God *does* seem to permit us to be placed in positions beyond our power, and in those cases the "way out" to which St. Paul refers will depend on the previous exercise of virtues such as mercy or humility, which will already have created the circumstances for salvation, if not of physical escape. Once again, Tolkien affirms that he did not impose his own solution on the story: it emerged from the characters themselves, and followed from the logic of their decisions. Thus, Frodo deserved all the honor he received on the Field of Cormallen. He had spent himself completely in the service of his mission. The sacrifices he had made had brought him to the destined point. Perhaps no one else could have got even as far as that (L 192).

And so, when Gollum bites the Ring from Frodo's finger and falls into the Fire, this is the consequence of Frodo's earlier (and freer) decision to spare Gollum's life. The salvation of the world, and of Frodo himself, is brought about in consequence of the pity and forgiveness that he had shown to Gollum earlier in the story (L 181). Thus in the end it is not Frodo who saves

Middle-earth at all, though he bore the Ring to the Mountain, nor Gollum, who took the Ring into the Fire. It can only be God himself, working through the love and freedom of his creatures, using even our mistakes and the designs of the Enemy (as *The Silmarillion* hints that he will do) to bring about our good. The scene is a triumph of providence over fate, but also a triumph of mercy, in which free will, supported by grace, is fully vindicated.

And what of Gollum? Even he is no cipher, no allegory or shadow only, but a fully three-dimensional character (beautifully realized, it has to be said, in the Peter Jackson movie). We are meant to pity as well as fear Gollum, and we do. We learn of his long existence as a slave of the Ring, which feeds on his petty desires, jealousies, and resentments, magnifying them into an artificial substitute for life, indefinitely prolonged. We know that he has committed evil deeds beyond count, yet we are shown the conflict that still torments him as the mercy shown by Frodo eats away at the foundations of his malice. One of the most moving scenes in the book, which caused Tolkien to weep as he wrote it, takes place on the stairs of Cirith Ungol as Gollum finds Frodo and Sam lying asleep, Frodo's head in Sam's lap, and peace in both their faces.

He reaches out a trembling hand to touch Frodo very gently.

> For a fleeting moment, could one of the sleepers have seen him, they would have thought that they beheld an old weary hobbit, shrunken by the years that had carried him far beyond his time, beyond friends and kin, and the fields and streams of youth, an old starved pitiable thing.

But Sam wakes to see him, as he thinks, "pawing at Master" and shouts at him roughly. The fleeting moment of grace passes beyond recall. Gollum's resolve to betray them is renewed, and he falls into the Fire still enslaved.

In Letter 181 Tolkien muses on the fate of Gollum, and the subtlety of his moral vision becomes evident. In his youth Sméagol had been broken by the Ring, but he would never have acquired it in the first place if he had not already made himself a thief and a murderer. Yet his will was still not totally corrupted many centuries later.

> By temporizing, not fixing the still not wholly corrupt Sméagol-will toward good in the debate in the slag hole, he weakened himself for the final chance when dawning love of Frodo was too easily withered by the jealousy of Sam before Shelob's lair.

He weakened himself, Tolkien says. Few writers are as conscious as this of the moral responsibility we each bear for our own fate. Tolkien allows his characters to make their own decisions for good or evil. Yet even so he does not judge them, for (as he adds) "we who are 'in the same boat' must not usurp the Judge."

The Return of the King

The immediate result of the Ring's destruction is the fall of the Dark Tower. In some very real sense, the Ring was the foundation on which the tower of Barad-dûr was built. Now its "towers and battlements, tall as hills ... great courts and dungeons, eyeless prisons sheer as cliffs, and gaping gates of steel and adamant" crumble and slide into the ruin of Mordor. All the paraphernalia of oppression, of politics for the sake of power, hang on one thing and one thing only: the thing symbolized by the Ring, now consumed by the Fire.

The victory of the allies follows swiftly. Their enemies are demoralized, scattered and witless. Aragorn is merciful and wise in judgment, and he enters the city of Gondor with a healing hand. His Coronation is itself an act of healing for the whole kingdom, bringing to an end the long sickness of Gondor and Arnor, the shadow of the Shadow upon Men.

Aragorn, the grim-visaged ranger of the wilderness who becomes King Elessar, is of course a type of King Arthur, and Gandalf a type of Merlin. In Aragorn, as in Arthur, the royal blood has to prove itself worthy of kingship by heroism. Arthur pulls the sword from the stone and founds the kingdom of Logres. Aragorn reforges "the sword that was broken," and reunites the two halves of the kingdom appointed to him, inaugurating a new age of the world. Merlin and Gandalf both function here as the representatives of Tradition, of the wisdom of the past—of memory, you might say. Both of them depart the kingdom once the legitimacy of the king has been established, the royal heritage transmitted.

Did Tolkien mean to suggest that Aragorn is the distant ancestor of Arthur? In chapter IX of Book V of *The Lord of the Rings*, Legolas mentions a prophecy that Lúthien's line will never fail. It seems possible. If these stories were originally intended as a mythology for England, it might have made sense to create an Elvish ancestry for the greatest king of Christian legend.

But the more important point is that in the story of King Elessar, and the other interwoven "kingly" motifs in the book, Tolkien is revealing profound truths about the royal authority that each of us must reinstate at the center of our own inner kingdoms, and the moral virtues of courtesy, courage, and chivalry that underpin that authority. Aragorn is a true king not only because of his lineage and the tokens of kingship he bears, but because he turns *back* from his royal quest to help the Hobbits, because of his years of selfless service as a ranger, because of his faithfulness to Arwen.

The King who is borne up by the tacit assent of his people, in whom all recognize the principle of justice tempered with mercy, whose authority flows from his humility before truth, is no doubt a rare man. *The Lord of the Rings* presents us with his portrait, an ideal portrait and thereby a guide to the pure principle of royalty. But the true King exists in the real world, as Tolkien knew. All the prophecies, all the types and shadows, Aragorn as well as Arthur, converge on Christ, King of a realm as wide as creation.

Aragorn rides the Paths of the Dead and frees the ghostly army of Oathbreakers from their curse by enlisting them against the darkness. At the Black Stone of Erech he unveils the standard of his realm that no man living can see, for it is night; but the living dead sense it, and follow. Jesus, of whom Aragorn is but a type or prefigurement in Tolkien's mythical history, enlists us in the "war of the Logos" (Rev. 19:11–21) by unveiling the standard of his own kingdom in the darkness of the Passion. Those who are spiritually dead, though they still walk the earth awaiting the fulfillment of prophecy, may recognize the love of God that reveals itself by descending; and follow it through death into a new day rising.

> On the throne sat a mail-clad man, a great sword was laid across his knees, but he wore no helm. As they drew near he rose. And then they knew him, changed as he was, so high and glad of face, kingly, lord of Men, dark-haired with eyes of grey.
>
> Frodo ran to meet him, and Sam followed close behind, "Well, if that isn't the crown of all!" he said. "Strider, or I'm still asleep!"

We too need the King to take his throne, in his "great castle, hundreds of miles away" (Butterbur). For then we can go back to our own polluted landscape, with its mean brick houses and its small-minded officials, its devastated orchards and avenues of trees. We can return there endowed with the authority of servants and friends of the King, to commence our own task: the task that awaits us at home.

The Scouring of the Shire

The great battles are over, the Ring of Power destroyed, and the King restored to the ancient throne of Gondor. Frodo and Sam have been honored on the field of Cormallen for accomplishing the quest. The Hobbits, transformed and ennobled, return to the Shire and must now defeat the unexpected evil that they find there.

> The Old Grange on the west side had been knocked down, and its place taken by rows of tarred sheds. All the chestnuts were gone. The banks and hedgerows were broken. Great wagons were standing in disorder in a field beaten bare of grass. Bagshot Row was a yawning sand and gravel quarry. Bag End up beyond could not be seen for a clutter of large huts.

The returning hobbits find their beloved homeland despoiled, polluted, and enslaved. The people of the Shire are now working for men who bully and exploit them, imprisoning any who break the numerous new rules and regulations. They are forced to live in poverty and fear, while the ruffians eat, drink, and smoke the fruit of the land. Traditional hobbit-holes are being replaced with ugly brick houses. In other words, the hobbits returned expecting to find again their secure, happy, rural community, and instead have come face to face with the industrial squalor of post-war England.

It is the exiled wizard Saruman who turns out to be responsible for all this, in a final act of revenge against the Hobbits who brought about the destruction of Orthanc. His headquarters in the Shire, and thus the center of the evil infection, is Bag End itself, Bilbo's, Frodo's, and (later) Sam's home, the heart of Tolkien's interior world.

The success of the hobbits in dealing with this final peril would not have been possible—would certainly not have been believable—if they had not experienced the epic adventure as a whole, and if we had not seen them transformed into heroes of song and legend; so that when they are plunged back into the banality of the Shire they are able to defeat the evil that they find with the grace—the gifts—that they have received in their travels. Those hobbits who have not been so initiated into heroism are helpless to oppose a force that enslaves by fear and the exploitation of self-interest. But the travelers have passed through darkness, in the Barrows, in Moria, in battle and in Mordor itself. The half-darkness of everyday evil holds no terrors for them. They have been broken and re-forged through service to others: to Frodo, to Théoden, to Denethor, to the peoples of Middle-earth.

Merry and Pippin, indeed, have been prepared in a special way for the task that now lies before them. Merry has been taken into Théoden's service, ridden with the Mark to aid Gondor, and aided Eowyn in the destruction of the Ringwraith whose breath causes despair. Merry's special gift, then, is the overcoming of despair and the raising of hope—signified by the ancient Horn of the Mark which is given to him by Éomer at their parting. Pippin has served Denethor the Steward of Gondor, Théoden's darkened image, learning to obey but also to transcend obedience when a higher good requires rules to be broken: in this case he is able to save Faramir whom Denethor has ordered to be burned while still alive.

When they return to the Shire it is Pippin who will tear up the "Rules" imposed by Saruman's men, and which the hobbits have passively accepted; while it is Merry who raises their hearts with the Horn of Rohan. Both of them have been prepared, also, by the direct assault on Saruman's Orthanc with the Ents: a rising of nature herself against the "mind of metal and wheels," as Treebeard calls him.

The biblical Book of Wisdom tells us: "the creation, serving you who made it, exerts itself to punish the unrighteous" (16:24). Saruman, trembling in his tower, illustrates the truth of these words.

> For not even the inner chamber that held them protected them from fear, but terrifying sounds rang out around them, and dismal phantoms with gloomy faces appeared.... The delusions of their magic art lay humbled, and their boasted wisdom was scornfully rebuked. (Wisd. 17:4, 7)

As the hobbits arrive in the Shire they meet one of Saruman's men. At Frodo's words, "The King's messengers will ride up the Greenway now, not bullies from Isengard," he merely sneers. This is too much for Pippin.

> "I am a messenger of the King," he said. "You are speaking to the King's friend, and one of the most renowned in all the lands of the West. You are a ruffian and a fool. Down on your knees in the road and ask pardon, or I will set this troll's bane in you!"

The scouring of the Shire is written not just as an account of the author's psychological and spiritual journey, but as a call to arms to the reader, as a blast on the Horn of Rohan summoning us to the help of our friends and the healing of our world. We too, if we have imaginatively accompanied the hobbits on this journey from the mundane to the epic and back again, are initiated into the realities that exist behind the veils of everyday life. Tolkien hints that a similar heroism is called for in us, as we see the England of our own day laboring under the disguised slavery of consumerism and overrun by half-orcs who despise our traditional way of life.

This is the heroism which expresses itself not by the sword (although strong action may indeed be called for), but by placing ourselves at the service of the Light in whatever way is demanded of us in our own circumstances. "I do so dearly believe," Tolkien wrote, "that no half-heartedness and no worldly fear must turn us aside from following the light unflinchingly."[7]

The Ring Today

Tolkien wrote a letter to his son Christopher in 1944. Referring to the news of his son's first solo flight with the RAF, so different from the silent skimming of the birds that Men dreamed of attaining when they sought to fly, he remarks: "There is the tragedy and despair of all machinery laid bare" (L 75).

Within *The Lord of the Rings*, Isengard under the wizard Saruman illustrates the "tragedy and despair" of reliance on technology. In the modern world, we have seen the devastating and dehumanizing effects of a purely pragmatic and quantitative approach to nature. The Romantic movement, from Blake and Coleridge to Barfield and Tolkien, believed there must be an alternative. Goethe even tried to lay the foundations for it: he called it a "science of qualities." At the end of his wonderful essay *The Abolition of Man*, C. S. Lewis writes of a "regenerate science" of the future that "would not do even to minerals and vegetables what modern science threatens to do to man himself. When it explained it would not explain away.

When it spoke of the parts it would remember the whole." And he adds:

> You cannot go on "explaining away" for ever: you will find you have explained explanation itself away. You cannot go on "seeing through" things for ever. The whole point of seeing through something is to see something through it. It is good that the window should be transparent, because the street or garden beyond it is opaque. How if you saw through the garden too? It is no use trying to "see through" first principles. If you see through everything, then everything is transparent. But a wholly transparent world is an invisible world. To "see through" all things is the same as not to see.[8]

Lewis here echoes Tolkien's concern with technology. He compares Francis Bacon with Marlowe's Faustus. For modern science and black magic alike the goal was power. Magic and superstition gave way before science mainly for pragmatic reasons: it proved to be more effective. But the "magician's bargain" tells us the price of such power over the forces of nature: our own souls. For, says Lewis,

> if man chooses to treat himself as raw material, raw material he will be: not raw material to be manipulated, as he fondly imagined, by himself, but by mere appetite, that is, mere Nature, in the person of his de-humanized Conditioners.

The conquest of nature turns out to be our conquest *by* nature, that is to say, by our own desires or those of others; and the Master becomes, in the end, a puppet.

In Letter 131 Tolkien contrasts the "magic" (technology) of the Elves with that of the Enemy: the goal of the former is Art, whereas the aim of the latter is "domination and tyrannous re-forming of Creation." The devices of the Elves are benign. They work with the grain of nature, not against it. Tolkien is not opposed to technology per se, but to the kind of technology that issues from a certain mentality of control. The desire for power, he writes, "leads to the Machine (or Magic)": the use of our talents or devices to bulldoze other wills.

The Ring of Power, the "One Ring to bring them all and in the darkness bind them," is a symbol or example of this kind of technology: the ultimate Machine. In making devices like the Ring to increase our domination of others, we inevitably make ourselves weaker by becoming dependent on them (L 211). They magnify our power but also externalize it, so that we ourselves wither by their use. When they are destroyed, that weakness is exposed. Sauron, when the Ring is destroyed, literally blows away on the wind.

The search for worldly control—power over nature and over others, which is to say "technological" and "psychological" power—is in the end self-defeating. The only true power is spiritual, and is exercised primarily over oneself. The ruler who first rules himself is also able genuinely to represent his people. He is not a man alone, but a man loved and supported by others. If he does not impose his own will upon his subordinates and thereby dissipate it, the will of his subordinates will flourish and support him. King Elessar is such a ruler. In the long run, a society built on respect and mutual support is always going to be stronger than a pseudo-society built on fear and self-interest.

Tolkien's most developed reflections on the nature of evil and the corruption of power can be found in *Morgoth's Ring*. Sauron may be the Dark Lord of the Third Age, but once he had been merely the servant and lieutenant of a much more powerful entity, Melkor, known to the Elves as Morgoth. Expelled from the world at the end of the First Age, Morgoth's shadow still lies across Middle-earth. In the section "Myths

Transformed," Tolkien reflects on the similarities and differences between these two figures.

Both make themselves vulnerable, ultimately, by seeking dominion. Morgoth acts through agents that he seeks always to control: armies, orcs, balrogs. For the sake of efficiency these must be made capable of acting to some extent on his behalf without having specific orders. Tolkien writes: "Part of his native creative power has gone out into making an independent evil growth out of his control." Sauron's weakness was due to the fact that he had placed a large part of his power into the Ring. But the power of Morgoth, originally much greater, has also gone out into a "Ring." Morgoth's Ring, Tolkien tells us, is the whole of Middle-earth, and his power runs even through the physical elements of which it is composed—including gold, apparently, more than silver. Water is one of the few elements that is almost entirely outside Morgoth's influence.

This explains the basis for the evil magic practiced by Sauron, for he is able to work with the "Morgoth-ingredient" in things, such as fire and gold in the case of the Rings of Power. It also helps to explain the general "taintedness" of Middle-earth (outside Lothlórien, which is specially protected). It explains the fact that nature is subject to disease and corruption, perhaps even to entropy, and it explains the world-weariness of the Elves, which is due not to their longevity so much as to the "tendency toward Melkor" inherent in earthly matter, including the matter of their bodies while in Middle-earth.

> Morgoth lost (or exchanged, or transmuted) the greater part of his original "angelic" powers, of mind and spirit, while gaining a terrible grip upon the physical world.... Sauron's, relatively smaller, power was *concentrated*; Morgoth's vast power was *disseminated*.

In "Myths Transformed" Tolkien also explains that whereas Morgoth's motivations are almost purely nihilistic, Sauron (very like the corrupt Saruman later on in the history) had no objection to the existence of the world as such, as long as it was under his control:

> He still had the relics of positive purposes, that descended from the good of the nature in which he began: it had been his virtue (and therefore also the cause of his fall, and of his relapse) that he loved order and co-ordination, and disliked all confusion and wasteful friction.

The empire of Sauron, then, is on a different scale, on a different order, from that of Morgoth, though by the concentration of his power Sauron becomes for a while stronger than Morgoth in the latter's "dissipated" phase. It is an empire that depends not only on slaves such as Orcs, but also on willing human vassals (Easterlings and others) who, for their own perceived advantage, or out of fear of reprisals, pay tribute to Mordor and even send armies to fight for Sauron when summoned to do so. Such arrangements are not uncommon among the "evil empires" of today.

How, then, should we treat such an enemy? Tolkien was always conscious of the temptation that besets the righteous: to employ an evil means in a good cause. This was how the great had fallen, how Gandalf and Galadriel might have fallen, and how we ourselves can still fall. The Easterlings are redeemable. What of Orcs, who were not made but only bred and corrupted by Morgoth? In "Myths Transformed" there is an interesting note. The Orcs, Tolkien writes:

> might have become irredeemable (at least by Elves and Men), but they remained within the Law. That is, that though of necessity, being the fingers of the hand of Morgoth, they

must be fought with the utmost severity, they must not be dealt with in their own terms of cruelty and treachery. Captives must not be tormented, not even to discover information for the defence of the homes of Elves and Men. If any Orcs surrendered and asked for mercy, they must be granted it, even at a cost. This was the teaching of the Wise, though in the horror of the War it was not always heeded.

Tolkien always insisted that his fantasy was not an allegory. Mordor was not Nazi Germany, or Soviet Russia, any more than it was intended to be Saddam's Iraq, or other more recent tyrannies. "To ask if the Orcs 'are' Communists is to me as sensible as asking if Communists are Orcs" (L 203). But at the same time he did not deny that the story was "applicable" to contemporary affairs, indeed he affirmed this. It is applicable not merely in providing a parable to illustrate the danger of the machine, but in showing the reasons for that danger: sloth and stupidity, pride, greed, folly, and lust for power, all exemplified in the various races of Middle-earth (see L 203).

Against these vices he set courage and courtesy, kindness and humility, generosity and wisdom, in those same hearts. There is a universal moral law, but it is not the law of a tyrant. It is the law that makes it possible for us to be free.

Thus the world Tolkien describes is our own, although he does so in the mode of fantasy, and the "very great story" he tells us is one that continues in our own day.

Chapter Four

A Hidden Presence: Tolkien's Catholicism

A letter to his friend Robert Murray, S.J., in December 1953 contains Tolkien's famous comment:

> *The Lord of the Rings* is of course a fundamentally religious and Catholic work; unconsciously so at first, but consciously in the revision. That is why I have not put in, or have cut out, practically all references to anything like "religion," to cults or practices, in the imaginary world. For the religious element is absorbed into the story and the symbolism. (L 142)

He goes on to say that this "sounds more self-important than I feel," for he has "consciously planned very little."

The Lord of the Rings is nevertheless Christian and orthodox in intention and spirit. It is permeated with a sense of eternity, of the objective order of good and evil, and of an all-wise providence (the sense that God somehow orders all things, even apparent coincidences): this is all part of that "forgotten sunlight" which serves to awaken us from the sleep of materialism. The spirit of courtesy that we see in Aragorn and Faramir, the respect for women and the determination to protect the weak, the virtues of courage and fortitude and prudence and justice that shine in these noble characters, are patterns of goodness that were learned from the Gospel.

Tolkien saw in the Christian revelation the meeting and fusing of legend and history, and in the Body of Christ the restored bridge from this world to the other. He persuaded

C. S. Lewis of this (though Chesterton's *Everlasting Man* was already an influence) during a walk in the grounds of Magdalen College, celebrated in Tolkien's long poem *Mythopoeia*. It was there that he turned on its head the old rationalist argument against Christianity—that it was "too good to be true," and must consequently be dismissed as a kind of wishful thinking. What if we wish it to be true because that desire has been planted in our nature by the One who made us? After all, the phenomenon of hunger proves the existence of food. Myths of a dying god resurrected or fairy-tales of healing and of virtue vindicated exist because we cannot help seeking what we were made to find. Nature was made for grace. Our hearts spoke true, and in Jesus Christ the Author of the world has once and for all vindicated those fleeting glimpses of "Joy beyond the walls of the world, poignant as grief," that art affords us.

Clearly Tolkien did not see himself as a religious writer in the same sense as Lewis. He did not feel called to enter the lists as a writer on Christian themes, let alone as a theologian or philosopher of religion. Nevertheless, with the posthumous publication in 1981 of his *Letters*, this side of his life was exposed to view, and it became clear the Catholic belief and sensibility he received from his mother and later from his guardian, Father Morgan, whom he called a "second father," permeated every aspect of his life.

The American Catholic Flannery O'Connor also wrote in a way that is not explicitly "religious." Like Tolkien, she wanted to portray the way grace and sin operate in the real world:

> This all means that what we roughly call the Catholic novel is not necessarily about a Christianized or Catholicized world, but simply that it is one in which the truth as Christians know it has been used as a light to see the world by.... The novelist is required to create the illusion of a whole world with

believable people in it, and the chief difference between the novelist who is an orthodox Christian and the novelist who is merely a naturalist is that the Christian novelist lives in a larger universe. He believes that the natural world contains the supernatural. And this doesn't mean that his obligation to portray the natural is less; it means it is greater. [9]

Flannery O'Connor had no desire to build alternative cosmologies on Tolkien's grand scale, but what she says about her own artistry applies as well to him as to herself. I am not claiming to judge Tolkien's degree of sanctity, but I do think he had what we today call a "spirituality," and that it shines through his writing. To a puzzled non-Christian, who tells him that he has created a world "in which some sort of faith seems to be everywhere without a visible source, like light from an invisible lamp" (L 328), Tolkien replies:

Of his own sanity no man can securely judge. If sanctity inhabits his work or as a pervading light illumines it then it does not come from him but through him. And neither of you would perceive it in these terms unless it was with you also. Otherwise you would see and feel nothing, or (if some other spirit was present) you would be filled with contempt, nausea, hatred. "Leaves out of the elf-country, gah! Lembas —dust and ashes, we don't eat that."

The Order of Grace

Tolkien's spirituality was, of course, deeply Catholic. And the first thing to note is that the specifically *Catholic* dimension of Christianity is almost entirely bound up with the Blessed Virgin Mary. The dogmas about Mary bring to a focus or "enshrine," if you like, everything that Catholics believe about the Incarnation and human destiny, about God's love for his creation and the way he intends to save it from death.

By giving Mary the title *Theotokos* (literally "god-bearer"), the early Church at the Council of Ephesus was not trying to elevate a mere creature above the eternal God, as though Mary had existed before God himself. The title was designed to contradict a popular heresy, to the effect that Jesus had been merely a human person, and only later (at the moment of his baptism in the Jordan) came to be inhabited by a divine spirit. What the Church wanted to say was that Jesus all along was a human being but not a human *person*.

The distinction presupposed a new understanding of human existence—one that we are still struggling to understand even today. The ancients knew that we are "natural" realities, like any animal, vegetable, or mineral. At the same time they could see that our mind and will are oriented toward the Infinite in a way that other animals seem not to be. This "supernatural" dimension reveals our rootedness in the Divine. The Jews and especially the early Christians went further than this. They knew that we are not only created by God, but also that we "face" God, because God has turned his own "face" (*persona*) toward us. In other words, we are not only rational beings, but *persons*. To say that in Christ a human (created) body and soul were assumed not by a human person but by a divine one is to say that, in Christ, the face that God turns to himself in the Trinity has become the face that God turns to us.

By being the mother of Jesus, Mary is necessarily the mother of a *person who is God*, not merely the mother of a human body assumed by God. At the same time, by giving her this title, the Church was defending the idea that motherhood cannot be adequately understood as a biological relationship alone, but is always "personal." A woman is not the mother of a body only, or of a human nature, but of a child; that is, always of a person.

This teaching about Mary had cosmic implications. The human nature of Jesus Christ does not exist in splendid isolation, but rather he takes flesh from a woman. That means he is joined to the material cosmos through his mother. Immediately he becomes vulnerable: what happens to the cosmos, happens to him, and vice versa. As God he has entered into it and bears it upon his shoulders; so that when he dies and is resurrected, and when he enters eternal life still in his (transformed) body, the material cosmos—*and first of all things his mother*—is also resurrected, and so can be assumed into heaven. Through the agency of the Holy Spirit, we are joined to this mystery and participate in it. Thus the dogma of Mary's Assumption, followed by her Coronation as Queen of the Universe (the final mystery of the Rosary, which Tolkien discusses in a footnote to Letter 212), though it marks her out as unique among all creatures, is paradoxically not something that isolates her from the rest of mankind.

The Eastern Church Fathers use the word *theosis* to describe this process, meaning "divinization" or "deification," and the Catholic *Catechism*, quoting Saint Thomas, says essentially the same thing (para. 460): "The only-begotten Son of God, wanting to make us sharers in his divinity, assumed our nature, so that he, made man, might make men gods." In other words, we are intended to become by grace what God is by nature, through participation in his eternal life of love. This precious message—the very heart of the Gospel—along with all that is intimately connected with it, is what is implied by the Church's teaching about the Virgin Mary.

With this as background, we can begin to understand why the Virgin Mary was at the center of Tolkien's spiritual life. For Catholics, the Virgin is the closest of all creatures to Christ. She is the fairest fruit and flower of creation, the one on whom all the divine gifts are lavished. Whatever Jesus Christ could do for human beings, he did first for his mother. She receives all graces; she is literally "full of grace." But divine grace is given only to be passed on, not to be hoarded. She therefore becomes the conduit for the graces that flow from her Son into the whole world. This is what Catholics mean by calling her the Mediatrix: she is the way the cosmos is joined to God.

To his friend Robert Murray, Tolkien wrote: "I think I know exactly what you mean by the order of Grace, and of course by your references to Our Lady, upon which all my own small perception of beauty both in majesty and simplicity is founded" (L 142). I have in my possession an undated letter from the Inkling George Sayer addressed to Felicitas Corrigan, O.S.B., in which Sayer reports that Tolkien had told him also that "I attribute whatever there is of beauty and goodness in my work to the influence of the Holy Mother of God." The woman whom Catholics call "Our Lady" is the center of a universe of beauty created by her Son. The natural beauties of landscape and forest, mountains and streams, and the moral beauty of heroism and integrity, friendship and honesty—all of which are celebrated in Tolkien's imaginative world—are gifts of God that come through her, and she is the measure of them, her beauty the concentrated essence of theirs.

For Catholics, the Virgin Mary has all the beauty that Eve lost, and just as Eve was the mother of all the living in the world that is past, she is the mother of the world to come. G. K. Chesterton captures this aspect of Our Lady in his poem "The Black Virgin":

> Clothed with the sun or standing on the moon,
> Crowned with the stars or single, a morning star,
> Sunlight and moonlight are thy luminous shadows,
> Starlight and twilight thy refractions are,

Lights and half-lights and all lights turn about thee.
But though we dazed can neither see nor doubt thee,
Something remains. Nor can man live without it
Nor can man find it bearable without thee.

Star of the Sea

There is another way in which Mary is present in *The Lord of the Rings*, and that is through her reflections in Galadriel and Elbereth. Galadriel is one of the pivotal Elvish characters: bearer of one of the three Rings untouched by Sauron and thereby the preserver of the land of Lothlórien. Tolkien himself calls her "unstained" in Letter 353 (a word that Catholics normally use only of the Virgin Mary), adding "she had committed no evil deeds." He admitted that Catholic teaching and imagination about Mary lay behind the character as portrayed in the novel (L 320). Yet the workings and reworkings of his manuscript reveal an ambiguity here, or at least an evolution, for in earlier drafts she was supposed to be a leader in the rebellion of the Elves against the Valar, the world's angelic guardians. If she was not entirely of Fëanor's party, she was drawn into league with him by a desire to rule lands of her own in Middle-earth.

From this rebellion or this ambition Tolkien later felt the need to absolve her. In Letter 320 (1971) he speaks of her having "proudly refused forgiveness" at the end of the First Age, but having been pardoned at the end of the Third because of "her resistance to the final and overwhelming temptation to take the Ring for herself." (The temptation, of course, played on her desire to rule.) Yet in the *Unfinished Tales*, we find a chapter containing the "History of Galadriel and Celeborn," in which Christopher Tolkien records the "late and partly illegible note" which is "the last writing of my father's on the subject...set down in the last month of his life." In this revised history, which he intended to incorporate into *The Silmaril-lion*, Galadriel is not at all involved in the rebellion of the Elves but indeed opposed it and was caught up in the departure from Aman to Middle-earth through no fault of her own. Thus she was morally as well as physically equipped to be the Elvish leader of resistance to Sauron in Middle-earth. We see here, I think, the pressure of the Marian archetype in Tolkien's imagination on the development of the character of Galadriel.

Not quite "immaculate" (without sin), then, in the official version, but to the Hobbits in *The Lord of the Rings* Galadriel is nevertheless a vision of wisdom, beauty, and grace, of light untarnished. Her parting gift to the dwarf Gimli is highly significant. He asks for a single golden hair from her head, which he intends to enshrine within imperishable crystal. In the Elder Days Fëanor had asked for a tress, and been refused three times, for her hair was famed for seeming to contain the light of the Two Trees. (The significance of this will be clearer after chapter 5.) Now she gives Gimli three hairs, one for each of her ancient refusals, which were bound up with so much grief for the Elves. Galadriel's gift heals the long rift between her people and the Dwarves. It implies that she now repents of any part her pride may have played in the long tragedy.

Galadriel, however, remains despite all of this an earthly figure. In Roman Catholic devotion and dogma, the Virgin Mary, having been assumed into heaven at the end of her earthly life, is venerated as Queen of Heaven and "Star of the Sea." We find this more cosmic aspect of the Marian archetype expressed in the person of Galadriel's own heavenly patroness, Elbereth, Queen of the Stars, who plays the role in Tolkien's *legendarium* of transmitting light from the heavenly places. It is to Elbereth that the Elves sing their moving invocation:

> O Elbereth! Gilthoniel!
> We still remember, we who dwell
> In this far land beneath the trees,
> Thy Starlight on the Western seas.

Tolkien would have been familiar from his childhood with one of the most popular Catholic hymns to the Virgin Mary, the tone and mood of which are markedly close to that of Tolkien's to Elbereth (see L 213):

> Hail, Queen of Heaven, the ocean star,
> Guide of the wand'rer here below:
> Thrown on life's surge, we claim thy care—
> Save us from peril and from woe.
> Mother of Christ, star of the sea,
> Pray for the wanderer, pray for me.

Starlight on the sea: for Tolkien a particularly evocative combination, as we have seen. Light shining in darkness, representing the life, grace, and creative action of God, is the heart of Tolkien's writing. Light, to him, is always in some sense feminine (remember that in Middle-earth the sun is referred to as "she"), and Mary the "universal mediatrix of grace" is present implicitly throughout creation. What is earthly beauty other than a light that shines in things and upon things, welling up from within, like the light in Galadriel's phial? The beauties of creation are not those of heaven, but they guide us to their Source as a star may guide us across the ocean: "For from the greatness and beauty of created things comes a corresponding perception of their Creator" (Wisd. 13:5).

In *Adventures in Orthodoxy*, Dwight Longenecker tellingly describes his reaction to a Raphael Madonna. "That Raphael painting was full of grace and truth, and I beheld its glory; and that's what Christians say about the relationship between Jesus and God [see John 1:14]. He is God's work of art. He incarnates beauty and truth." Implicit here is the notion that beauty is *not* exclusively, as we have been told so often, in the eye of the beholder. It lies beyond ourselves, in a sense "ahead" of us. It is where, deep down, we all want to get to, though we know we have a long way to go. "That's why we all feel that beauty takes us outside ourselves and puts us in contact with something greater, more mysterious, and more wonderful than we thought existed before," Longenecker goes on.

> As I gazed on that luminous Madonna, I made contact not only with something beautiful, but with Beauty. It was also an astoundingly intimate experience of purity and power. For a moment I glimpsed a kind of purity that was both as soft as moonlight and as hard as diamonds. I suddenly realized that purity, like all things beautiful and refined, is an acquired taste. Like the fragile beauty of a Mozart aria, or the calm, exquisite beauty of a Chinese vase, purity can be fully sensed only by those who pursue purity themselves, and this realization made my own sordid and tepid life seem small. While looking at the naked child and the Madonna's mysterious smile, I also realized that purity is a hidden and subtle virtue—a precious thing, available only to those who have been given the eyes to see. [10]

There is an echo in this splendid passage of Sam's description of Galadriel to Captain Faramir, in which Catholics recognize their image of the little girl from Nazareth, crowned with flowers and stars:

> Beautiful she is, sir! Lovely! Sometimes like a great tree in flower, sometimes like a white daffadowndilly, small and slender like. Hard as di'monds, soft as moonlight. Warm as sunlight, cold as frost in the stars. Proud and far-off as a snow-mountain, and as merry as any lass I ever saw with daisies in her hair in springtime.

Lady Day

Towards the end of *The Lord of the Rings*, when the Ring has been destroyed and Sauron's work undone, Frodo is lying in bed recovering from the ordeal, talking with Gandalf. In Gondor, the wizard tells him, "the New Year will always now begin upon the twenty-fifth of March when Sauron fell, and when you were brought out of the fire to the King."

Tom Shippey was the first to point out in this connection that March 25 is the Christian feast day that celebrates the Annunciation: the day when Christ was conceived in the Virgin's womb. It is celebrated with readings that describe Mary's meeting with the Angel Gabriel and her "yes" to God. This used to be called Lady Day, and was indeed the first day of the year in many parts of Europe. It is exactly nine months before Christmas, because of the time required from the Virgin to come to term and bear her Son.

In some traditions it is also held to have been the date of the Crucifixion. John Saward cites the following wonderful passage from Honorius of Autun:

> This day is numbered among the chief festivals, because the beginning of the whole Christian religion is dated from it. On this day the world ruined by sin was restored to life by the Passion of Christ. On this day, too, John the Baptist was beheaded, and on this day James, the brother of John, had his head chopped off. On this sacred day, as the whole Church today celebrates, the Incarnation of Christ was announced by an angel. We read that on this day, at the very hour when the first man was created in paradise, the Son of God, the New Man, was conceived in the Virgin's womb. She was the Paradise of fruit, the *fons hortarum*, because in her sprang forth the Tree of Life, and from her the fount of wisdom flowed forth and poured out all its delights, in whom are hid all the treasures of wisdom and knowledge (cf. Col. 2:3).[11]

Why then did Tolkien choose March 25 for the destruction of the Ring? Well, think again about what the Ring represents. We have already considered it as the archetypal "Machine." Viewed theologically the Ring of Power exemplifies the dark magic of the corrupted will, the assertion of self in disobedience to God. It appears to give freedom, but its true function is to enslave us to the Fallen Angel. It corrodes the human will of the wearer, rendering him increasingly "thin" and unreal; indeed its gift of invisibility symbolizes this ability to destroy all natural human relationships and identity, to become untouchable by light.

The person who places himself within the golden circle of the Ring seeks not to be seen, and thereby to have power over others. In this respect it resembles the Ring of Invisibility in the second book of Plato's *Republic* (where Plato interestingly contrasts the "unjust man" who uses the Ring to steal from others with a "just man" who is not corrupted by the power it gives, and who ends up being crucified). Through the magic power of the Ring we escape the limitations of matter to enter the world of spiritual forces, but in the very act of doing so we become horribly visible to the forces of evil.

In fact the Ring is partly a symbol of the sin of pride. It draws us toward the Dark Lord by tempting us to become like him. Its circular shape is an image of the will closed in upon itself. Its empty center suggests the void into which we thrust ourselves by using the Ring. Once there, unseen by others, we are cut off from human contact, removed from the reach of friendship or companionship, anonymous and isolated. The power that the Ring gives is an illusion. It takes us, ultimately, into a world where we are alone with the Eye (the Eye that can see only reflections of itself). In that world of evil there is no room for two wills: the wearer is either absorbed and destroyed, or he defeats Sauron and becomes another Dark Lord himself.[12]

The Ring is sin itself: tempting and seemingly harmless to begin with; increasingly hard to give up and corrupting in the long run. Its destruction, therefore, is a figure of the great reversal of sin achieved at the Annunciation when Mary welcomed the Word of God into our world. Her *fiat*, "Let it be to me according to your word," overturns the refusal of God's will that we call original sin. That sin also resulted in a kind of invisibility, as Adam hid from the Lord in the forests of Eden: "But the Lord God called to the man, and said to him, 'Where are you?'"

In the National Gallery in London is a small panel painting known as the Wilton Diptych. Commissioned by Richard II, it is one of the most precious and mysterious works of art in England. It shows the king kneeling, surrounded by saints, offering the nation to the Virgin Mary, or perhaps to the baby Jesus who is in her arms, reaching out to receive it. The king is surrounded by a barren and forbidding landscape; but at the feet of Mary the ground is green with grass and bright with flowers,[13] just as the air around her is thronged with angels.

This is the Mary who is ever-present to Tolkien, at the center of his imagination, mantled by all natural beauty, the most perfect of God's creatures, the treasury of all earthly and spiritual gifts. What Elbereth, Galadriel, and other characters such as Lúthien and Arwen surely express is precisely what Tolkien said he had found in Mary: *beauty both in majesty and simplicity*. Majesty, for here we see beauty crowned with all the honors that chivalry can bestow; and as for simplicity, well, what is more simple than starlight?

A Sacramental Universe

We have seen how the "religious element"—and even the Catholic element—is absorbed into the symbolism of the stories. But did Tolkien go too far in eliminating religion? Some readers have found it strange that there is seemingly not even any *Pagan* religion present in Middle-earth,[14] which is after all set in pre-Christian times. Occasional invocations of Elbereth and the Númenorean grace or "Standing Silence" before meals hardly constitute a religion.

To this, too, Tolkien had an answer. The Men of the West described in his stories, he says, descended from those who tried to repent of the original Fall, and who deliberately fled the influence of the Prime Dark Lord, escaping from Paganism (in the sense of polytheism) and satanism (the worship of Morgoth) into pure monotheism. For them only Eru was to be given worship, as he was in the far West by the Valar and the Eldar; but no religion could be built around the Valar, and for Men at this time Eru was too remote to be the focus of some ritual form of worship: he had not yet revealed (as he would reveal later to the Jews) how they could build a covenantal relationship with him (L 156). (More detail is supplied in a footnote to Letter 153.)

Tolkien was very careful in trying to construct his world in a way that would faithfully echo the wisdom of the true Creator, as he understood God to be, yet without anticipating the specific content of the Christian revelation. For that revelation had not yet taken place, and "the Incarnation of God is an *infinitely* greater thing than anything I would dare to write" (L 181).

Within *The Lord of the Rings* (and even within *The Silmarillion*), Tolkien stuck consistently to this principle. The Marian symbolism we have been looking at is no departure from it. It causes no offense to "Pagan" readers, for whom the references to a Lady of the Stars, and the other images of beauty and grace that we find scattered throughout the story, need refer only to an "eternal feminine" or a goddess of light. As for the Catholic who knows what the author really intends by these evocations, there should be no difficulty regarding them as examples of mediated divine action in the distant past, for the Catholic lives in a symbolic cosmos, in which everything—every stone, every flower, every neighbor—both exists in its own right and symbolizes some aspect of the divine.

As Tolkien wrote in 1955 to W. H. Auden: "Each of us is an allegory, embodying in a particular tale and clothed in the garments of time and place, universal truth and everlasting life" (L 163). In this sense the entire natural world is what we might call "sacramental"—not a sacrament in the strict theological sense, but nevertheless a symbolic system apt for the communication of spiritual realities. "God speaks to man through the visible creation," says the *Catechism of the Catholic Church* (para. 1147). "Light and darkness, wind and fire, water and earth, the tree and its fruit speak of God and symbolize both his greatness and his nearness."

The great exponent of this natural sacramentality is the French Jesuit Jean-Pierre de Caussade (b. 1675). He writes:

> God's love is present in every creature and in every event, just as Jesus Christ and the Church inform us that the sacred body and blood of God are truly present in the Eucharist. His love wishes to unite itself with us through all that the world contains, all that he had created, ordained, and allowed. That is his supreme purpose, and to accomplish it he uses both the best and the worst of his creatures, the most unpleasant and the most delightful of happenings.[15]

In this way, God speaks to us through what happens, moment by moment. Even before the birth of Christ, everything that exists and everything that happens has its root in God and is a "word" in the divine language. A sense of divine providence, of things meaning more than we know, of coincidences needing to be understood, is of course one of the strongest and most lasting impressions we receive from *The Lord of the Rings*.

The seven sacraments themselves are of course instituted by Christ much later in time than the events being narrated and so cannot be directly implied. The divine self-communication in cosmos and history culminates in the Incarnation of Christ, whereby the created world is assumed and healed from within by God himself. The sacraments are symbolic structures that make this Incarnation accessible to the members of the Church. Nevertheless, even these are hinted at within the story. Tolkien justified this by noting: "far greater things may color the mind in dealing with the lesser things of a fairy-story" (L 213). In this case of *lembas*, the Elvish "waybread" that nourishes the will even more than it does the body, and that is more potent when received after fasting, the "far greater thing" that has influenced Tolkien's story is the Blessed Sacrament, the Eucharist that makes it possible for Christ himself to enter our lives in the form of food.

Tolkien's personal devotion to the Eucharist was intense. He would try to attend Mass each day. (While in Oxford, this would be either at St. Aloysius, then in the hands of the Jesuits but today the Oratorians, or the Church of St. Gregory and St. Augustine further up the Woodstock Road.) He writes to his son Michael: "The only cure for sagging or fainting faith is Communion.... Frequency is of the highest effect. Seven times a week is more nourishing than seven times at intervals" (L 250). Earlier he had written this moving testament:

> Out of the darkness of my life, so much frustrated, I put before you the one great thing to love on earth: the Blessed Sacrament.... There you will find romance, glory, honor, fidelity, and the true way of all your loves on earth, and

more than that: Death: by the divine paradox, that which ends life, and demands the surrender of all, and yet by the taste (or foretaste) of which alone can what you seek in your earthly relationship (love, faithfulness, joy) be maintained, or take on that complexion of reality, of eternal endurance, which every man's heart desires.

Marriage

It is significant that this passage on the importance of the Eucharist comes at the end of a long letter (L 43) full of advice concerning another key sacrament in Tolkien's life: marriage. There he warns his son against the over-idealization of these things, and even against the aspiration to find one's "soul-mate" which has led so many men and women, married and unmarried, into grief. He admits that his own case is exceptional, but hints that even so he is not unacquainted with the frustration and unhappiness that can occur within the best of marriages.[16] Most marriages, even the happiest, can be called "mistakes" in the sense that (theoretically at least) a more suitable partner might have been found. At one time or another it is likely that tensions will arise. What the married person has to realize is that his "soul-mate" is not some theoretical alternative partner, or even some real person who is met tragically "too late," but quite simply the person he is *actually married to*.

The importance Tolkien attached to marriage as a state, and as a spiritual path in life, is evident also in another long letter he drafted to C. S. Lewis, responding to Lewis's suggestion that there should be two sorts of marriage: on the one hand binding Christian wedlock and on the other a civil marriage that could be dissolved if necessary. He argues that the Christian teaching on marriage (that it should be "monogamous, permanent, rigidly faithful") cannot be compared to the

Muslim teaching on the non-consumption of alcohol, which Lewis had chosen as an example of a religious rule that ought not to be imposed on everybody. Christian marriage and chastity is not a specialized custom or discipline for the few; indeed, if it were not a natural and healthy way for all human beings to live it would be "an intolerable injustice" to impose it even on Christians (L 49).

In the 1920s another of the Inklings, though an Anglican, had written a defense of indissolubility in *Outlines of Romantic Theology*. Charles Williams there described marriage as not merely a social contract but a "means of the work of redemption." Divorce "is an attempt to nullify a sacrament actually in operation." "It is not that it ought not to happen; for Christians it *cannot* happen, whatever formula is pronounced or ceremonial enacted. When the work is once begun, for better or worse it cannot be stopped." The "work" is that of mutual sanctification, which can be achieved only by some form of "utter surrender"—marriage being one such form.

Marriage occupies an interesting position in the "sacramental economy" of Christianity, being a sacrament that Christ did *not* institute but simply restored. In the Catholic view, it was created in Paradise, since Adam and Eve were literally made as "one flesh" in the beginning, before the Fall. Divorce was later permitted by Moses as a concession to the weakness of human nature, but abolished by Jesus (in Mark 10:2–12), who came to perfect the law and to supply the grace needed to fulfill it as God had intended. The Catholic Church permits both separation and annulment, but the latter only on the grounds that no true marriage had in fact taken place. That could happen only if one or other partner had not meant or been able to mean the words of the marriage vow, which are carefully chosen to express the *total consent to union of life* that enables God to join together the couple into a new sacramental entity.

Tolkien mentioned in his letter to Lewis that at one time he had "*dissented* in feeling" (though not expressly) from the teaching, and only later come around to appreciating the rightness and the wisdom of it—along with the danger to society in permitting or encouraging any other standard of behavior. By 1943 the rightness of the teaching was self-evident to him—so much so that it applied even to Elves. During the 1950s he composed a text called "Laws and Customs among the Eldar" (to be found in *Morgoth's Ring*), which included details of the marriage customs in Valimar. There we read among other things that "Marriage is for life, and cannot, therefore, be ended, save by the interruption of death without return." The Elves, of course, may be killed, but unlike human beings this constitutes for them merely an interruption of earthly life, to which they may return. In that case the re-incarnate is the same person, and the marriage union remains in existence. (The delicate and complex case of second marriages is explored in considerable detail for those who want to take this further.)

Marriage and the Eucharist do not merely happen both to be at the heart of Tolkien's spiritual and moral life: they are intrinsically related, as Charles Williams explains very beautifully in *Romantic Theology*. The union of divine and human natures in Christ at the moment of his conception is itself appropriately called a kind of "marriage"—being a union that does not dissolve but rather depends upon the distinction of the two elements. Furthermore the passion of Christ on the cross is a "marriage" of Christ with his spouse the Church (see Eph. 5:32). It signifies the total self-giving of Christ, culminating in the gift of the Holy Spirit of love, which he breathes out with his dying cry in the darkness of Calvary. From this sacrifice of God and Man on the cross, present in the Eucharist, the Holy Spirit is poured out into the world, making the many one.

The Heart of a Child

In 1969 Camilla Unwin, daughter of the publisher, wrote to Tolkien in connection with a school project to ask him about the purpose of life. In answer, he took her first through the argument for God's existence (L 310). Of all the approaches people have adopted to this question, the one that appeals to him most is perhaps predictable, given his interest in creativity: it is the "argument from design." The world is full of patterns, seeming to proceed from an endlessly creative fountain of invention. But is there truly a mind behind all this? If there is not, then the world is not there for a purpose at all. But if there is, then our knowledge of that mind can be increased by contemplation of it. Perhaps the purpose of our lives is "to increase according to our capacity our knowledge of God by all the means we have, and to be moved by it to praise and thanks."

And so we arrive at the heart of Tolkien's spirituality, which he sums up in the *Gloria in Excelsis*: "We praise you, we call you holy, we worship you, we proclaim your glory, we thank you for the greatness of your splendor." He continues:

> And in moments of exaltation we may call on all created things to join in our chorus, speaking on their behalf, as is done in Psalm 148, and in the Song of the Three Children in Daniel II. PRAISE THE LORD... all mountains and hills, all orchards and forests, all things that creep and birds on the wing.

This touching letter to a child seems to me to say a great deal about the author. His spirituality was one of gratitude and praise—inevitably also a spirituality of childhood, for only the childlike person can truly praise and glory in the wonders of creation that have become so stale to the elderly. In his essay "On Fairy-Stories" Tolkien cites with approval Andrew Lang's comment: "He who would enter into the Kingdom of Faerie should have the heart of a little child." The Virgin Mary, who was so central to Tolkien's spiritual life, shows us how to have the heart of a child. She was, as Georges Bernanos writes, "younger than sin." It is innocence and gentleness, purity and trust, which make us young. The mind withered by cynicism and regret cannot appreciate nature as it comes fresh each day, each moment, from the hand of God. In the words of G. K. Chesterton's *Orthodoxy*,

> It may not be automatic necessity that makes all daisies alike; it may be that God makes every daisy separately, but has never got tired of making them. It may be that He has the eternal appetite of infancy; for we have sinned and grown old, and our Father is younger than we. ("The Ethics of Elfland")

The pure in heart will see God, Christ tells us in the Sermon on the Mount, and the pure are the young. Tolkien remained "young" enough to write stories for his children and tell them with relish, young enough to chase tourists out of his garden on occasion dressed as a Anglo-Saxon warrior, and young enough to see and love the stars and the leaves in his garden as things that God does not tire of making.

I do not know how closely Tolkien had studied the life of St. Philip Neri, the founder of the Oratory to which his guardian Fr. Francis Morgan belonged, but the spirituality we can discern in his own life and writings was very close to that of the saint of joy to whom God gave a "heart of fire" in 1544. Like St. Francis more than three hundred years earlier, St. Philip was a playful, childlike, musical saint.[17] Undoubtedly we can place Tolkien, through Fr. Morgan, in this very clear line of spiritual paternity. Cardinal Newman, too, belonged to it, being the founder of the English Oratory. The way of life of the Oratorians, who were priests living together in community yet not bound by a religious Rule—in some ways a "collegiate" existence not unlike that of Oxford and Cambridge, though founded on personal friendship—particularly appealed to Newman. As a married layman, Tolkien's life took a different path, but as an Oxford don, a devout Catholic, and a lover of poetry and music, there are more than a few Oratorian resonances in his life.

Another Catholic saint whose spirituality resembles that of Tolkien is the most popular modern "saint of holy childhood," the Carmelite nun Thérèse of Lisieux. Both Tolkien and Thérèse believed that sanctity can be attained not necessarily, or not only, by the great deeds of mortification and renown with which saints are normally associated, but by the following in fidelity of a "little way" through daily life, a way set beneath our feet by God. This is again quite similar to the spirituality of Caussade. "The road goes ever on and on...," in the words of Bilbo's walking song, and for Tolkien it is the walking of the road in hope that matters, relying entirely on God's help rather than one's own strength. "At any minute it is what we are and are doing, not what we plan to be and do that counts" (L 40).

This is Frodo's unassuming kind of heroism, as he volunteers to take the Ring "though I do not know the way," as he picks his way through the Dead Marshes, and through Shelob's tunnel in total darkness. At times he needs literally to be carried by Sam, as Thérèse said she needed to be carried by God, a small child lifted by her mother or father, up steps that she cannot manage on her own. The Carmelite spirituality of the "dark night" seems particularly appropriate for Frodo in

Mordor, and that blind despair in which he staggers toward Mount Doom, no longer able to visualize or remember light, or fresh water, or any natural beauty.[18]

Frodo is no saint, in the strict sense. Nor are many whose mission takes them through the land of shadow. For them there may be no savor of victory, and even success may feel like a living death. They have been "too badly hurt." Yet even unlooked for, in the weariness beyond all conscious hope, the sun may rise. For Frodo, watching from a ship that sails above the bent world, "the grey rain-curtain turned all to silver glass and was rolled back, and he beheld white shores and beyond them a far green country under a swift sunrise."

Chapter Five

Let These Things Be

Tolkien's "Middle-earth" is firmly rooted in the "Midlands" of England. The elements, animals, and plants of nature are vividly and lovingly portrayed. His letters, as well as his stories, reveal a man profoundly sensitive to the beauties of the natural world. Here is an example, describing a frosty garden in Oxford after Christmas:

> The rime was yesterday even thicker and more fantastic. When a gleam of sun (about 11) got through it was breathtakingly beautiful: trees like motionless fountains of white branching spray against a golden light and, high overhead, a pale translucent blue. It did not melt. About 11 p.m. the fog cleared and a high round moon lit the whole scene with a deadly white light: a vision of some other world or time. It was so still that I stood in the garden hatless and uncloaked without a shiver, though there must have been many degrees of frost. (L 94)

Patrick Curry, in his book *Defending Middle-Earth,* links Tolkien's spirituality to his love of nature. Certainly Tolkien's book was taken up during the 1960s and 1970s by the hippies and the Greens opposed to what they called the "military-industrial complex," and this contributed to its dismissal by the literary establishment as a "cult book."

At the same time, Tolkien portrays nature as animated and enchanted in a way that seems at odds with the view normally associated with Christianity. Indeed Curry, who is not a Christian, praises him for this neopagan quality. While the descriptions of forests and plains, mountains and storms, changes of light and season, are described so realistically that readers feel they have actually visited the landscapes of Middle-earth in the flesh, there is also a sense that more is going on here than meets the eye. The fox who, "wandering through the wood on business of his own," stopped and sniffed at the hobbits sleeping under a tree in the open air, remarking to himself, "There's something mighty queer behind this" (in the chapter "Three Is Company") may have wandered in from another kind of story. Nevertheless it is clear that in Middle-earth birds can be both messengers (of Radagast, for example) and spies (of Saruman), while the very trees—at least in Fangorn and the Old Forest—can move and talk, and the air and water are full of spiritual presences.

It is not entirely fair to accuse the Christian Church, as many still do, of having felled the "sacred groves" of Europe. Nor can Christianity be blamed for the ecological crisis, for the instruction in Genesis to "fill the earth and subdue it" need imply nothing more than the exercise of a prudent and priestly stewardship over nature. In many cases the new churches deliberately preserved earlier sacred sites, as Pope Gregory explicitly advised St. Augustine of Canterbury to do in England. The idea was that the ancient spirits previously appeased (in some cases) by human or animal sacrifice must now "bend the knee" to Christ, and their energies must be channeled into the worship of One who came to save nature, not destroy her. The systematic assault on nature had to await a modern era and a new justification.

G. K. Chesterton's biography of St. Francis of Assisi explains how the coming of Christianity meant that nature was no longer to be worshiped,[19] but could now be loved in a new way, at least by those who most profoundly understood the true message of the Gospel. "Man has stripped from his soul the last rag of nature worship, and can return to nature." It may have been necessary to topple some idols and to cleanse some temples, but by the time of St. Francis the "flowers and stars have recovered their first innocence. Fire and water are felt to be worthy to be the brother and sister of a saint."[20] It is this Franciscan spirit that permeates Tolkien's writings—and we recall that St. Francis and his disciples did on occasion speak to the animals as though they could understand, as did many of the Celtic saints. (Gandalf's fellow-wizard Radagast the Brown, the friend of birds and animals, seems to be a very clear image of St. Francis—and we know that Tolkien loved Assisi.)

In order to understand the natural world as Tolkien portrayed it in *The Lord of the Rings*, we need to go deeper and read *The Silmarillion*. Tolkien himself felt he had "been forced to publish up-side-down and backwards," and that it would be important for his readers eventually to have things in the right order (L 191). *The Silmarillion* should come first. A bit like an Elvish Old Testament, it is a collection of documents of varying provenance and style, held together roughly in historical sequence. Yet it has a beauty and a splendor of its own that seems to emerge best when read aloud, either to oneself or to others. It was, after all, conceived as the product of a tradition in which the stories would have been sung as poetry. The deluge of Elvish names that immediately engulf the reader form an essential part of the book's charm, for, as we have seen, the root of Tolkien's poetic vision is the language he devised and the thrill of the music that he sensed in words. We are just lucky that we do not have to read the whole work in Elvish, which is what the author would have preferred!

The names, therefore, are very far from being arbitrary labels devised to enable the reader to differentiate the different characters. They have a power of their own when spoken. To most of us, names are opaque; but if we were to read them with Tolkien's sensibility, each would open up for us an interior landscape, evoking the magic of first participation, wherein all things were more transparent to the Word by which they were created.

The Music of Meaning

In order to establish the ultimate framework of his *legendarium*, Tolkien composed a creation myth. This is of more than incidental interest: not only does it contain some tremendous writing, but it is also the key to understanding the mythology as a whole.

In making this account of the Beginning of Days, Tolkien drew upon many legends that were known to him and upon the Jewish and Christian traditions that he believed to be true. He was trying to write an account that would be complementary to, while not contradicting, the Genesis story. Any differences from the biblical account were supposed to be due to the fact that it was written not from the human point of view, but from that of the Noldorian Elves through whom it had been transmitted to Bilbo and Sam at Rivendell.

For Tolkien, as a Catholic, God is the Creator of the world *ex nihilo* ("out of nothing"). The world has not always existed. It was not made out of some pre-existing substance. It is not made out of the body of God, in some way divided or parceled out among creatures. It is not made by two gods. All of these alternatives have been firmly rejected by the Christian tradition. The orthodox teaching is clear: the world—indeed *any conceivable world*—can have been made only by the One God from nothing. (Even an everlasting world would still need God to bring it ever into existence.) In both the Bible and

The Silmarillion, the physical world is created by the Word of God. In the Elvish account, however, there are three preceding stages, the first of which involves the creation of the Ainur, or "Holy Ones." The second stage is the proposing of themes and the singing of a great music by Eru and the Ainur together.

I suppose the central importance Tolkien gives to music (as does C. S. Lewis, if you recall Aslan singing Narnia into existence in *The Magician's Nephew*) may have been suggested to him by some famous lines in the Book of Job. "Where were you...when the morning stars sang together, and all the sons of God shouted for joy" (Job 38:7), God asks Job in the Authorized Version—or "when the morning stars praised me together, and all the sons of God made a joyful melody" in the Douay-Rheims translation familiar to Catholics of Tolkien's generation. At any rate, as Verlyn Flieger remarks in *Splintered Light*, for Tolkien, combining the creative principles of Genesis and the Gospel of John "Light and music are conjoined elements made manifest in the visible world sung as the Music of the Ainur."[21] When Sam remarks on arriving in Lothlórien, "I feel I was *inside* a song, if you take my meaning" (quite apart from the fact that "inside a song" is the exact meaning of the word "enchanted"), he utters a more profound truth than he consciously realizes.

Tolkien's "Ainulindalë," the Elves' account of the creation of the world, begins as follows:

> There was Eru, the One, who in Arda [the Earth] is called Ilú-
> vatar; and he made first the Ainur, the Holy Ones, that were
> the offspring of his thought, and they were with him before
> aught else was made. And he spoke to them, propounding
> to them themes of music; and they sang before him, and he
> was glad.

Melkor, the highest and most gifted of the Ainur (equivalent to Lucifer in Christian terminology) begins to rebel, by interweaving "matters of his own imagining that were not in accord with the theme of Ilúvatar; for he sought therein to increase the power and glory of the part assigned to himself." The discord spreads through the music until it resembles a raging storm. In response, Ilúvatar intervenes three times. The first time he smiles as he introduces a second theme into the music, but Melkor again prevails, and frowning he introduces a third theme, "at first soft and sweet, a mere rippling of gentle sounds in delicate melodies; but it could not be quenched, and it took to itself power and profundity." This is the theme of Elves and Men, the "Children of Ilúvatar." The third and final time that Ilúvatar intervenes, as Melkor's discord drowns out both new themes, is in order to end the music.

Eru then translates the music into the form of a great vision, displayed in the void. Now the Ainur are able to see the meaning of the music they have been making. They see how it can be embodied in a world of living creatures, interwoven destinies, composed of elements and forces unfolding in time. The Ainur are drawn toward this newly created world by a love of beauty.

> [They] looked upon this habitation set within the vast spaces of the World, which the Elves call Arda, the Earth; and their hearts rejoiced in light, and their eyes beholding many colors were filled with gladness; but because of the roaring of the sea they felt a great unquiet. And they observed the winds and the air, and the matters of which Arda was made, of iron and stone and silver and gold and many substances; but of all these water they most greatly praised. And it is said by the Eldar that in water there lives yet the echo of the Music of the Ainur more than in any substance else that is in

this Earth; and many of the Children of Ilúvatar hearken still unsated to the voices of the Sea, and yet know not for what they listen.

Knowing the desire in the hearts of the Ainur for this beauty to become "real" in the same way that they are themselves, Eru sends forth the Secret Fire and kindles the world into actuality with the divine command:

> "*Eä!* Let these things Be! And I will send forth into the Void the Flame Imperishable, and it shall be at the heart of the World, and the World shall Be; and those of you that will may go down into it."
>
> And suddenly the Ainur saw afar off a light, as it were a cloud with a living heart of flame.

Verlyn Flieger, ever conscious of the importance of words for Tolkien, writes that "*The Silmarillion* is testimony to his desire to 'explore the implications of one word,' for the whole vast sweep of his mythology is in truth just that—the exploration of the implications and ramifications of the one word *Eä.*"[22]

But how does this account square with the one we find in the Book of Genesis? (On this topic, see also Appendix Seven.) For Tolkien, God's act of creation can be broken down into four stages:

1. thought (the Ainur),
2. music (which also involved the angelic fall),
3. light in the void (when the music is translated into vision), and finally
4. being, or material existence.

On the other hand, the Genesis account starts as follows:

> In the beginning God created the heaven and the earth. And
> the earth was without form, and void; and darkness was
> upon the face of the deep. And the spirit of God moved upon
> the face of the waters. And God said, "Let there be light": and
> there was light. And God saw the light, that it was good: and
> God divided the light from the darkness. (Gen. 1:1–4, AV)

The main point of Genesis is identical with that of the
Elvish account: that there is One God, who is the sole and
supreme Creator of all things seen and unseen. Notice that
even before God's word pronounced over the face of the deep
causes light to spring into existence, there is mention of three
other "things" in Genesis, if we can call them that, which seem
already to have been made by God:

1. heaven (or "heaven-and-earth"),
2. earth (a formless void), and
3. the "waters" over which the Spirit of God is moving.

If there is a direct correspondence to each of these in Tolkien's account it is probably to:

1. the Ainur,
2. the formless void that surrounds them, and
3. the song.

Of these the song is perhaps the most intriguing. If the deep
mentioned in Genesis is the primordial substance of creation,
the sea of potentiality, then the music of the Ainur could be
said to be the pattern of vibration created on the surface of the
deep by the "spirit" of God. And so we "hearken still unsated to
the voices of the Sea" and know not for what we listen.

Another biblical account of creation is found in the Prologue to the Gospel of John:

> In the beginning was the Word, and the Word was with God, and the Word was God. The same was in the beginning with God. All things were made by him; and without him was not any thing made that was made. In him was life; and the life was the light of men. And the light shineth in darkness; and the darkness comprehended it not. (John 1:1–4, AV)

Here John deepens the earlier account of creation. Genesis speaks of "the spirit of God," but it is unclear whether this is a separate divine person from the "God" referred to in the first sentence. John, on the other hand, speaks of the "Word" (Greek: *Logos*) who is "with" God yet also "is" God, and this is intended as a reference to the divine nature of Christ, the Son of God. *Logos* also means "harmony," "order," and "meaning."

For Christian theology, based on the events recorded in the Gospels and reflection upon these by the early Christians, God is one divine "substance" yet three divine persons. Father, Son, and Spirit are each the same God, yet distinct from each other in a way that does not divide them into three separate things. Tolkien's account cannot be explicitly trinitarian, for it is supposed to pre-date the Christian and even the Judaic revelation. What it does instead is explore "behind" God's act of creating the *World That Is*, and find there a spiritual creation preceding the physical. The corporeal world embodies a vision, the vision embodies a music, and the music is the harmony of the Ainur, who are the offspring of divine thought.[23]

The Gods of Middle-earth

The Elvish account of creation is close to some versions of Platonic cosmology, but it should be noted that each succeeding stage, though it manifests the one before it, is no mere "echo" or diminished reflection of the one before—as it might be in a scheme that described the world as some kind of automatic emanation from God, radiating out into the void. At each stage God *adds* something that was not there before. The music is something "proposed" to the Ainur, in which they have the freedom to express their own natures and even to try to rebel. The vision leaves the Ainur "amazed." The world, again, is more than the vision: "and they knew that this was no vision only, but that Ilúvatar had made a new thing: Eä, the World that Is." It is real, now, in the same sense that they are.

In an unfinished letter (212 in the published collection), Tolkien describes this as differing somewhat from most Christian accounts of the Creation, in that the angelic fall takes place before the creation of the material world, and consequently a tendency to evil is able to enter into the world "already when the *Let it Be* was spoken" by Ilúvatar. However, the fall of Lucifer to become the "Satan" normally identified with the serpent in the Garden is only hinted at, never described in the Bible. The Christian (and Jewish) tradition has embellished the account of Genesis, using other hints scattered throughout Scripture (including the reference of Jesus to having seen Satan fall "like lightning from heaven"), but it never definitively established whether the angelic fall took place before or after the creation of matter. Lewis and Tolkien had therefore speculated that a prior, angelic fall would help to explain the great sufferings we observe in nature, which are hard to attribute entirely to the fall of man.

Tolkien, of course, has no doubt that evil is the result of free decisions by a created nature that was good at the outset. Matter itself, and the natural world, are both originally good, albeit corrupted. Furthermore, while the evil that is done by Melkor may destroy the original design of the Creator and mar the creation at every level, the eventual victory of Ilúvatar is certain, for even the work of the Fallen One will somehow prove "a part of the whole and tributary to its glory." Ilúvatar tells them that "no theme may be played that hath not its uttermost source in me, nor can any alter the music in my despite. For he that attempteth this shall prove but mine instrument in the devising of things more wonderful, which he himself hath not imagined."

The Ainur who descend to play the parts they have chosen within the history of Earth, contending from the outset against the chaos introduced by the dark Angel, are called Valar (Powers). They are accompanied by numerous attendant spirits called Maiar, some of whom later have key roles in Middle-earth (Sauron, Gandalf, Saruman). The sky god Manwë is the chief of the Valar and closest to Ilúvatar. Paired with him is Varda or Elbereth, the goddess of light and Lady of the Stars. Ulmo is the Lord of Waters, dwelling alone in the oceans and rivers. Aulë is the Lord of material substance and the "smith" of the gods; he is paired with Yavanna, the Giver of Fruits and goddess of growing things, known to the Elves as Queen of the Earth. The others include the warrior god Tulkas, the hunter Oromë, and Mandos, who is the keeper of the Houses of the Dead.

Resemblances to the Roman and Greek pantheon and the Norse gods of Asgard are obvious: Zeus, Poseidon, Ares, Hades, and several others are present and accounted for. (A detailed comparison with the Norse gods is given by Marjorie J. Burns in *Tolkien and the Invention of Myth*.) But the differences are striking too. The old gods' rough edges have gone, the lustful squabbling of the Olympians and the Aesir is notable for its absence, and the presence of a supreme deity beyond even Manwë is explicitly affirmed. Manwë himself (unlike Zeus) "has no thought for his own honor, and is not jealous of his power, but rules all to peace." In other words, Tolkien has integrated the ancient Pagan conception of deity with a Christian understanding of the world. His implied proposal is that the supposedly more ancient Elvish "histories" contain more accurate information about the gods than many of the mythological guesses made by man.

Tolkien's pantheon embodies, in concentrated form, his poetic insight into the natural cosmos. As such it repays not only close attention, but repeated meditation. In some sense he may have actually believed in these Powers, or at least something like them. Certainly he had a basis for doing so in Christian teaching about the Nine Choirs of Angels (Seraphim, Cherubim, Thrones, Dominations, Virtues, Powers, Principalities, Archangels, and Angels). The Roman Catholic tradition is firm on the existence of a hierarchy of created spirits or Intelligences that are involved (always under God's overall direction or orchestration) in the building and administration of creation. The modern *Catechism of the Catholic Church* reaffirms this tradition. In fact the Church teaches that one of the lesser spirits is assigned to every human being as a guardian and guide through life and as a companion after death: Catholics are encouraged to pray to their guardian angel every day, and Tolkien most probably did so.

A rare glimpse of this essentially private type of experience is afforded by a letter (L 89) in which he describes a vision he received while praying before the Blessed Sacrament in a traditional devotion called the "Forty Hours." He perceived a speck or mote suspended in the Light of God. The mote was himself, "or any other human person that I might think of with love," and the experience was accompanied by a great sense of joy. The mote was glittering white in the ray connecting it to the source of Light, and that ray was nothing less than the Guardian Angel of the mote, the expression of God's living attention directed toward that particular person. In another letter (54) he writes of the guardian angel as supporting us, as it were "from behind," giving us the strength to face God freely for ourselves, like a spiritual umbilical cord or life-line.

This sensitive awareness of the angels is reminiscent of John Henry Newman, whose sermon on "The Powers of Nature" is a beautiful evocation of the role of the Ainur in the world we see around us, operating behind the phenomena observed by science.

> I affirm, that as our souls move our bodies, be our bodies what they may [according to science], so there are Spiritual Intelligences which move those wonderful and vast portions of the natural world which seem to be inanimate....Every breath of air and ray of light and heat, every beautiful prospect, is, as it were, the skirts of their garments, the waving of the robes of those whose faces see God in heaven.[24]

For Tolkien and other members of his circle the angels are like Plato's Forms (Justice, Man, Rose, and so on), but they are *alive*; they have *free will*.[25] As living creatures distinct from the divine Essence, they pre-exist the world of time—which simply means that the world is made to exist through an act of God that includes them as secondary causes in its shaping and composition. The freedom of the angels means that they can turn against God. The very structure of the world becomes a drama of freedom and choice.

The concept of living ideas can perhaps be traced to the Pythagoreans, for whom Numbers were living gods. The music of the Ainur is probably equivalent to the "music of the spheres" in this long tradition. But there is a great profundity in the novel idea introduced by Tolkien that the angels themselves, in his account, *do not hear the end of the music*, but must await its fullfilment along with the whole creation.

The beauty of what God is to accomplish in world history surpasses the harmony of the spheres itself.

Ages of Light and Darkness

The Powers who choose to enter into Arda as "Valar" initially shape it according to their own conceptions of beauty, taming its tumults and making of it a "garden for their delight." With the arrival of Melkor, however, they are forced to strive for mastery, and the world is torn and shaken, losing its early symmetry. Aware from the Music that the Children of Ilúvatar (Elves and Men) are destined to arise in the course of time, the Valar need to make it safe for these more fragile creatures. Unwilling to risk excessive damage to the fabric of Arda, therefore, they allow themselves to be driven into the West, where they build up the land of Aman, the city of Valimar, and the great mountain of Taniquetil crowned with stars.

Much of the later drama is shaped by this "retreat" of the gods from the center of the world into the West. There is some suggestion in the posthumously published writings that Tolkien believed this to be a "mistake" of the gods, showing a lack of faith in Ilúvatar. If they had known all that would befall as a result of abandoning Middle-earth to Melkor at a crucial time in its history they would have held their ground. Of course, as we know, even the mistakes and misjudgments of the gods are worked by Ilúvatar into his greater design. The gradual removal of the numinous world of the gods from Middle-earth, until it is finally taken away from the realm of the Visible altogether, seems by hindsight an inevitable process. We stand at a later point in the Music, and its design has begun to be revealed to us. However, the gods were not compelled to adopt the course they did. Like us, but in their own higher sphere of action, they had the freedom to do otherwise.

We are now out of the Ages of Creation and into a later but still "prehistoric" or mythical period, each successive age of which is named after its main source of light. For as Verlyn Flieger has revealed so clearly, the concrete metaphor of Light and its history gives an underlying structure to Tolkien's mythos. The light of Arda comes first from two great Lamps, raised by the gods above the north and the south of the world. After these are cast down by Melkor, only Aman is illuminated, this time by the gently modulated radiance of two Trees grown by the song of Yavanna—first a silver tree called Telperion and then a golden called Laurelin, their liquid light being hoarded in "great vats like shining lakes."

While the Trees still shine in Aman, the Age of the Stars begins in Middle-earth. Varda/Elbereth now sets new and brighter stars and constellations in the sky, made from the silver dews of Telperion, as light for the children of Ilúvatar when they awake. In his impatience to see the Children, Aulë makes intelligent creatures of his own: the Seven Fathers of the Dwarves. He is rebuked by Ilúvatar, who nevertheless grants the Dwarves the independent life and free will that is his to give. (For Tolkien the creation of a soul is always a direct intervention of God, akin to the first making of the world itself.)[26] When the Elves at last arise silently on the shores of Cuiviénen, hearing the sound of running water, the stars are the first things they see: "Therefore they have ever loved the starlight, and have revered Varda Elentári [Star-kindler] above all the Valar," and they associated this forever with the sound of water. (Elves can see perfectly well by starlight.)

The Elves are known as "those that speak with voices" (Quendi). As Treebeard points out, it is they who begin to name things and to devise language. The language they invent is itself a response to light—fitting enough in a world that begins with the unity of music, light, and *Logos* (Word). Against the background of Owen Barfield's theory of the evolution of consciousness, Verlyn Flieger writes: "Consciousness and self-consciousness, manifest in speech, express the Elves' relationship to light" (p. 76). We would also do well to recall the fact that the phenomenon of light remains mysterious even today, that is, even to modern science. The optics of Isaac Newton was based on the splitting of white light into many colors (a departure, as Gandalf emphasizes to Saruman, from the path of wisdom). But when Einstein built his theory of relativity around the fact that the speed of light remained constant no matter what the velocity of the observer, the old Cartesian/Newtonian mechanistic understanding of light had effectively been transcended. In 1951 Einstein wrote that after fifty years of thinking about it, he was no closer to understanding what light actually is—*nor was anyone else.*

This "absolute" quality of light in modern physics recalls aspects of the medieval and ancient view of light as the primal form of corporeity and the expression of the first divine Word. The medieval world was built out of light, and this light was understood as an expression of God's creative act of "seeing." The poetic thrill we feel when a modern astronomer tells us that the elements of our bodies are made from stardust, having been forged in the heavenly furnaces millennia ago, is surely a faint echo of that ancient insight. Until the modern period, too, it was commonly assumed in a tradition that derived from the Greeks that the human eye saw by virtue of a spiritual fire or light residing within it, which rayed out to meet and merge with the light of the world. Tolkien writes from within that tradition. Eyes glowing and shining, as I remarked before, is more than an overused metaphor: it fits a mythology that is, among

other things, an account of the entwined history of light, consciousness, and language.

With the arrival of the Elves, we have come also to the
creation of the "Silmarils," which give their name to the saga
as a whole. These holy jewels represent an incarnation of the
light that comes from heaven, in a form that can be grasped
by creatures of the earth. Their maker, Fëanor, a prince of the
Noldorian Elves and their greatest craftsman, fills them with
liquid light from the Two Trees in Valinor. What is most desirable about the Silmarils is not therefore their crystalline form
but the light that lives in them, which is itself not a creation of
the artist but a gift from the gods. Fëanor's "greedy love" for the
work of his hands (they represent, after all, the highest point
attainable by both art and science) marks the Fall of the Elves,
for "sin" involves attempting to take possession of such gifts,
and forgetting to hold them in trust and gratitude. If the drama
of time is the use and misuse of freedom, the jewels are at the
center of that drama.

The Fall of the Elves is expressed outwardly in the stealing
of the Silmarils by Melkor, now named "Morgoth," the Enemy.
At the same time the Trees are destroyed, sucked dry and poisoned by the spider-creature Ungoliant, personification of
Morgoth's envy: the desire of darkness for the light. The radiance of the Trees remains only in the Silmarils, which Fëanor
and his sons vow to pursue with vengeance and hatred to
the end of the world, withholding them even from the Valar.
This terrible oath turns them also against the other Elves, and
drives them into exile. Middle-earth is now center stage. It is
there that the drama continues to unfold, and it does so under
a new dispensation of light, for the Moon and Sun are fashioned from the last fruit of the dying Trees, and three long Ages
of the Sun begin: the First Age revolving around the defeat of

Morgoth, the Second the rise and fall of Númenor, and the Third the War of the Ring.

These three cycles each express the fate of light on a new level. We are moving, if you like, from mythical toward historical time, and in consciousness from the primal unity toward a fragmented, externalized universe. Men arise for the first time under the light of the Sun. Their early years are unknown to the Elves and therefore not recorded.[27] In the First Age of the Sun, the Silmarils are regained but then placed beyond reach, while the memory of the ancient light enters the bloodstream of Men through Beren and Eärendil. In the Second Age, the pursuit of the light still lingering in the West becomes confused with earthly glory. After the drowning of Númenor, Middle-earth is cut off from the West and all it represents. In the Third Age, the interior light now hidden in the bloodline of the Dúnedain must emerge through the destruction of the Ring that threatens to engulf it, becoming the spiritual foundation for an Age of Men.

It is worth noting that the conception of time demonstrated here is both cyclic and linear. Each cycle repeats certain themes and patterns, but with important variations, just as might occur in a musical composition. From one point of view we see nothing but declension from an initial state of purity and concentration; from another we see a series of advances in complexity. Both points of view are enfolded within an ordered unity that can be perceived only as beautiful, when it is grasped as a whole, as a *gestalt*.

Owen Barfield believed that the European tradition had broken from the repetitive cycles we find in the world of ancient myth and ritual largely thanks to the Hebrews. While the Greeks had discovered form in space, the Hebrews had discovered form in time. Through the Jewish and Christian tradition God had revealed a linear pattern in history. It was no longer simply an earthly copy of some heavenly archetype, it was *going somewhere*. Myth gave way to history. But Barfield added that only modern consciousness had made the mistake of assuming a narrative must be *either* a historical record *or* a symbolical representation, thus eliminating the cyclic element altogether. For Barfield and Tolkien the best narratives were both.

Death and Immortality

The many stories in *The Silmarillion* from the three Ages of the Sun are largely concerned with another theme, as important as that of the history of light, which emerges particularly strongly in the contrast between Men and Elves. The new theme is *death*, and the various ways of escaping or accepting it (see L 212). Tolkien, of course, had a particularly strong sense of mortality, thanks to the early death of his parents and his experience of the war in which he and C. S. Lewis lost most of their close friends. This personal fascination with the meaning of death helps to endow his mythology with a seriousness and even urgency that is rare in fantasy writing. He was wrestling with a universal human concern, and consequently his mythology becomes a vehicle to explore the human condition itself.

Tolkien realized that the yearning for the Light from which we came, for a lost Golden Age, an age of innocence, is intimately connected with the desire for immortality. The sense of universal entropy, of falling away, of sliding into decay, of losing one's greatness, of becoming old and grey, is all part of the "taste" of death. Our desire for immortality is not really for that slow decline to be even slower. It is not, when we get right down to it, a desire to be merely *extended*, to be spread like a small piece of butter over too much bread (to use Bilbo's analogy). The Ring promises an immortality of that kind, but a life of servitude to the Ring is no better than a living death. The real desire for immortality, on the other hand, is healthy; it is a desire to overcome the process of decline itself. It is a desire not to extend but to *transcend* time.

A great many people these days believe in reincarnation. They believe it in the form originally taught by the Theosophical Society: the soul moves from body to body in order to educate itself and to evolve beyond the human state, eventually liberating itself entirely from matter and becoming one with the universal Spirit or Cosmic Consciousness. The idea of "liberation from matter" is reminiscent of the ancient heresy of Gnosticism, but it has a particular appeal to Westerners who since Descartes have been accustomed to thinking of the mind as a ghostly passenger or pilot in the machine of the body and, since the nineteenth century, of all life in a continual process of evolution. It also appears to many people as an attractive and merciful alternative to the Christian teaching that we have only one life and only one chance to escape the eternal fires of hell.

In its original Asian form, the theory of reincarnation was both more complex and less consoling. Reincarnation *as a human being* was regarded as an extremely rare chance. If that life was squandered by bad living, a second chance was not the immediate result: more likely would be a series of lifetimes in one of the hells or as one of the lower animals. In Buddhist versions of the teaching, it is not so much metaphysical as therapeutic, designed to enlist the imagination in a process of progressive detachment from desire.

In any case, even the popular doctrine of reincarnation is not as consoling as it first appears. A person who believes in reincarnation is often unable to find much comfort after the death of a loved one in the idea that the beloved is once again an infant and has completely forgotten his previous life. Deep down, we all want something rather different: a continuation of personality and of relationships.

Christians who wish to accommodate a belief in reincarnation are obliged to reject the clear teaching of the saints and assume that the Gospels (in which Christ speaks of an eternal hell as a real possibility) must at some point have been deliberately falsified. Reincarnation is therefore incompatible with Catholic, Orthodox, or Evangelical Christianity, which take seriously Christ's promise that his Spirit will remain with the Church until the end of time, guiding it into the truth. Tolkien, as a practicing Catholic, must have found Barfield's acceptance of the doctrine one of the more bizarre aspects of his devotion to Rudolf Steiner.

Tolkien did not, however, see anything wrong with exploring the idea in the world of his imagination and made good use of it in constructing the drama of the Elves. The Elves are immortal, in the sense that they do not die of old age or illness, and if murdered can be "sent back" from the Halls of Mandos to resume their life on earth. Their fate is not to depart from the world, but to remain for as long as it exists, if not in fully embodied form, then in a kind of limbo or waiting state. Only when the world itself ends would they face the great mystery of what lies beyond Time; but for the whole life of the world they are bound within it, and can be parted from their bodies only temporarily.

At first Tolkien assumes the Elves' normal way of return will be by being reborn as children. However, in later writings this changes. Tolkien was perhaps too conscious of the way our embodiment within a family and a set of relationships helps to make us who we are. Reincarnation would imply too great a change in the *hröa* (body) of the elf to be consistent with real self-identity. Tolkien concluded that his return must be in the form of resurrection rather than reincarnation. The "resurrection body" would be a kind of thought-form, based on the memory of his first embodied state. It would be able to pass through matter at will, but it could also become tangible if desired.

The temptation of the Elves is always to a kind of melancholy, for the Elves are the great appreciators and stewards of nature, but being blessed with an unfailing memory they are also burdened with a sense of transience and loss. Their music reflects this, because music is an art of transience and change, and their songs express both a love for the patterns of time and an attempt to capture, celebrate, and repeatedly invoke them. As time goes by the weight of memory increases, and correspondingly the importance of the present and the future seem to dim. (The Elves "remain until the end of days, and their love of the Earth and all the world is more single and more poignant therefore, and as the years lengthen ever more sorrowful.") Men, on the other hand, look mostly to the future, and their temptation is not to halt time but to extend it—to conquer it, ultimately, by manufacturing more and more: by postponing death in every way possible.

Ilúvatar has decreed that the destiny of Men lies somewhere else, a mystery both to the Elves and to themselves. "Therefore he willed that the hearts of Men should seek beyond the world and should find no rest therein." Christians will recognize here an echo of St. Augustine's famous phrase; "Thou hast made us for Thyself, and our hearts are restless till they rest in Thee." But one important divergence from the usual Christian description of reality should be noted, namely, that death is here no punishment for Original Sin, but a great gift and an inherent part of the nature of Man.

Writing in 1954, Tolkien himself seems unsure whether or not this could be construed as heretical (L 156), but by 1958 he had arrived at an explanation that seemed to satisfy him. In Letter 212 he writes that the account of death in the Silmarillion reveals *the Elvish view* of how human death should be viewed, even if it was originally inflicted on Men as a punishment. Once accepted, any divine punishment—which is, after all, intended as a blessing, for it corrects a fault—can also be seen as a "gift." The Creator is, after all, supremely creative, and when forced by the rebellion of his creatures to alter the design of the world (in this case by imposing the punishment of death as a consequence of human sin), he will bring out of that change a new and perhaps an even greater good.[28]

The fate of Men is to leave the world behind after a brief life and not to return as the Elves do, but to continue into a mystery that is "more than memory." The last king of Númenor rejects this fate, and, seeking an impossible immortality, sets foot on the shore of the Blessed Lands, bringing down catastrophe upon his people. The earth is made round, so that the sea-road to the West never reaches it but returns in a circle to the place where it began. The Elves will now be able to sail the Straight Road from Middle-earth to Valinor only by a special grace of the Valar.

The drowning of Númenor in Tolkien's famous recurrent dream was an important source of his inspiration. That image is also one of the purest and most powerful images of death and loss in all of literature. Drowning by an unstoppable wave is the speeded-up version of the Thing that faces all of us, though we contrive to forget it for a while.

Given its centrality in Tolkien's mythology as the link between the world of today and the Elder Days when the world was flat, between mythical time and historical time, the drama of Númenor and its progeny lies at the heart of his work. Shaped like a great five-pointed star, the island known as the "Land of Gift" represents the mingling of earth and heaven in the midst of the sea—another image of buried and fragmented light. But the tragedy of Númenor points in two directions: forward and back. Forward lies the story of Aragorn and Arwen, familiar from *The Lord of the Rings*. For Aragorn is the heir of Elendil, leader of the survivors from Númenor. He bears on his brow the "Star of the Dúnedain," which recalls his ancestor Eärendil, the father of the first king of Númenor, Elros, the brother of Elrond. But backward, behind both these stories, lies the tale of Beren and Lúthien, and with this we come even closer to the source of Tolkien's inspiration.

Set in the First Age, the story tells how love first binds together Man and Elf. In brief, Beren, a mortal man, falls in love with Lúthien, the daughter of the Elf-King Thingol and Melian, one of the angelic Maiar who had entered Arda in the beginning with the Valar. To get rid of this unwelcome and unworthy human suitor, Thingol sends him on an impossible quest: to bring him a Silmaril from Morgoth's crown. On his way to recover the holy jewel, Beren is cast into a pit by Morgoth's lieutenant Sauron, to be devoured by werewolves. Lúthien, however, has followed after him (contrary to every stereotype of passive womanhood) and rescues him with the aid of her ancestral magic and Huan, the hound of the Valar. The three achieve the quest together: it is Lúthien who captivates Morgoth and puts him to sleep while Beren cuts loose the Silmaril. Together they escape from Morgoth's fortress only to be confronted at the gate by its most dreadful guardian:

the wolf Carcharoth, who swallows the hand that holds the Silmaril and later slays Beren himself.

The tale continues. Lúthien follows Beren to the underworld of the dead and sings to the Lord of Death, Mandos himself, the most beautiful song in the world, a song that weaves together the griefs of the Two Kindreds. If the world is founded on song, this is its central theme. Moved to tears, Mandos appeals to the Lord of the Valar to make an exception to the normal rules that separate the destinies of Men and Elves. For love of Beren, Lúthien has rejected the fate of the Elves in favor of a human death, in order to be with him forever. Her decision will open the way for others, including Arwen, to choose the same destiny. The couple is rewarded with a brief return to life in Middle-earth before their final journey into the unknown. In time they died once more, although "none marked where at last their bodies lay."[29]

The second marriage of Elves and Men takes place in Gondolin. Idril is the daughter and heir of Turgon, ruler of the hidden Elvish kingdom. Tuor is a man chosen by Ulmo, the Power of the Waters, to bear a prophetic message to Gondolin about its peril. But Turgon does not heed the warning, and Gondolin is betrayed from within—the last of the Elvish kingdoms in Middle-earth to fall. Its spectacular destruction by a massive assault of orcs, dragons, and balrogs was one of the first parts of the *legendarium* composed by Tolkien and was eventually published in the second part of the *Book of Lost Tales*. Idril and Tuor with their son Eärendil escape from the destruction of Gondolin down to the coast, where they join the people of Elwing, grand-daughter of Beren and Lúthien, to whom Eärendil is soon wedded.

Eärendil and Elwing sail to the West for aid, leaving their sons Elros and Elrond in captivity. Thanks to the Silmaril that

Elwing has inherited, and his remarkable triple ancestry from gods, Elves, and Men, Eärendil is permitted to land in Valinor (though he will never be permitted to return) and to plead before the Valar on behalf of all the free peoples of Middle-earth. His plea is answered, and the Valar descend upon Middle-earth in a war of wrath that destroys the power of Morgoth.

The Silmaril is set upon the brow of the immortal Eärendil as he sails the darkness of space in a silver ship fashioned for him by the Valar. It is in this form, as a beam of light from the Morning and Evening Star, captured in a crystal phial, that the same light much later comes to Frodo as a gift from Fëanor's cousin Galadriel. The two remaining Silmarils, at last retrieved from Morgoth's crown, are stolen from the Valar by the surviving sons of Fëanor, only to be buried in the sea and in the fires of the earth at the end of the First Age.

From this overview we see the way Tolkien evoked the tragedy and the mystery of death against the backdrop of the greater mystery of existence itself. The sense of loss, of a world passing away, fills *The Lord of the Rings* and *The Silmarillion* like the sound of the sea and the glimmer of starlight; but for there to be loss, there must first have been possession. The destruction of the Trees, the successive falls of Menegroth, Nargothrond, Gondolin, and Númenor, leading to the removal of Valinor, add layer upon layer to the mood of nostalgia evoked by Galadriel in the song she sings to Frodo, a song of the Noldor in exile:

> Now lost, lost to those from the East is Valimar!
> Farewell! Maybe thou shalt find Valimar.
> Maybe even thou shalt find it. Farewell!

It is a nostalgia for something real. Through myth, through poetry, Tolkien has evoked a feeling beyond words that comes from the deepest levels of our nature, a yearning that God has implanted within us. That feeling is a sign that we are called back to a Light, Music, and Word that contain and transcend the pattern and the meaning of the world. The Elves can hope for nothing higher than memory: a frozen image of perfect beauty in the Far West. And if Tolkien had not been a Christian, perhaps this would have been something like his final word. But Men are not Elves, and the hope of Men does truly reach further.

"In sorrow we must go, but not in despair," Aragorn tells Arwen. "Behold! we are not bound forever to the circles of the world, and beyond them is more than memory." The death of Man involves a definitive departure from this world into an unknown future. When it becomes a choice—for Lúthien, for Arwen—it is an act of faith in the Maker of all things, and in the love he has placed within the human heart. In the end only the Creator can triumph over Morgoth, whose will precipitates the tragedy of the fall. This he will do, *The Silmarillion* hints, not by forcing the free will of his creatures, but by weaving their own failures and sins into a yet greater design of his own.

Chapter Six

Behind the Stars

The Light of Valinor (derived from light before any fall) is the light of art undivorced from reason, that sees things both scientifically (or philosophically) and imaginatively (or subcreatively) and "says that they are good"—as beautiful.

—J. R. R. Tolkien to Milton Waldeman (L 131 fn)

What Tolkien sensed behind the folklore and languages of the North and in fragments of Anglo-Saxon poetry can be given a name: it is "Elvishness." Like "Orcishness" this is an element in human nature, these two contrasting strands representing the spiritual possibilities of humanity in our own time.

> The Elves represent, as it were, the artistic, aesthetic, and purely scientific aspects of the Humane nature raised to a higher level than is actually seen in Men. (L 181)

At one level, then, the Elves represent an ideal way of relating to the natural world. They are artists, but also scientists and nature-mystics: they have a love, intense and intimate, for the trees and flowers, the hills and rivers, the winds and sounds of this earth, which they cherish, celebrate, and try to preserve with their magic.

Tolkien traced Elvishness back to the point where Elves and Men first come together: "The story of Beren and Lúthien," he writes (L 156 fn), "is the way by which 'Elvishness' becomes wound in as a thread in human history." In this chapter I want to examine Elvishness—what it is, what it meant to Tolkien, how it is wound into our own nature, and what it might mean to us now.

Elvish Aesthetics

The desire to see Elves, like the desire to see a dragon, is not merely a desire to see a particular kind of exotic creature but (as we have seen) a desire for Faërie, the world, realm, or state in which such creatures have their being. If we really found a fire-breathing lizard in a zoo, that would be very boring: not what we are looking for at all. The other realm is desired precisely because it is "imaginary." It is desired because of something we find there, of which the very substance of that world is somehow composed. Some have called this "magic," but (for reasons explained above) Tolkien prefers the word "enchantment." It is not an escape from reality.

> *Faërie* contains many things besides elves and fays, and besides dwarfs, witches, trolls, giants, or dragons: it holds the seas, the sun, the moon, the sky; and the earth, and all the things that are in it: tree and bird, water and stone, wine and bread, and ourselves, mortal men, when we are enchanted.

The secondary world of imagination is made, in fact, out of the primary world, and—this is the key point—it reveals or "makes luminous" the things of which the primary world is made.

> By the forging of Gram cold iron was revealed; by the making of Pegasus horses were ennobled; in the Trees of the Sun and Moon root and stock, flower and fruit are manifested in glory.

Chesterton tells us in *Orthodoxy* that fairy-tales founded in him the conviction "that this world is a wild and startling place, which might have been quite different, but which is quite delightful" (the "feeling that something has been *done*," that every color, every leaf, every creature is "dramatic"). Similarly, Tolkien tells us that in fairy-tales he "first divined the potency of the words, and the wonder of the things, such as stone, and wood, and iron; tree and grass; house and fire; bread and wine" ("On Fairy-Stories").

The realm of Faërie is an imaginary world, which is to say that it is made from images of real things as a pot is made of clay or a painting is made of paint. Yet we go there seeking a light that we cannot find in the primary world. The action of making or experiencing such a world is in part a creative act; we are in fact claiming our birthright to "make by the law in which we're made"; made, that is, "in the image and likeness of a Maker." The imaginal is where we sense most strongly the essence of creativity, of the divine imagination that conceives and gives life to the primary world. It is where words are born. It is the world where things could be other than they are, or not be at all, and where *what they are* is seen as for the first time, because it is seen against a background that looms much closer in Faërie: the background of pure light, or pure darkness.

With this in mind, let us read the description of Lothlórien as Frodo experiences it. It is well worth going back to *The Lord of the Rings* to read it in full, and in context. I think it evokes an intense, almost mystical experience that lies close to the heart of the book.

> It seemed to him that he had stepped through a high window that looked on a vanished world. A light was upon it for which his language had no name. All that he saw was shapely, but the shapes seemed at once clear cut, as if they had been first conceived and drawn at the uncovering of his eyes, and ancient as if they had endured for ever. He saw

no color but those he knew, gold and white and blue and green, but they were fresh and poignant, as if he had at that moment first perceived them and made for them names new and wonderful. In winter here no heart could mourn for summer or for spring. No blemish or sickness or deformity could be seen on anything that grew upon the earth. On the land of Lórien there was no stain.

Though he walked and breathed, and about him living leaves and flowers were stirred by the same cool wind as fanned his face, Frodo felt that he was in a timeless land that did not fade or change or fall into forgetfulness. When he had gone and passed again into the outer world, still Frodo the wanderer from the Shire would walk there, upon the grass among *elanor* and *niphredil* in fair Lothlórien.

They entered the circle of white trees. As they did so the South Wind blew upon Cerin Amroth and sighed among the branches. Frodo stood still, hearing far off great seas upon beaches that had long ago been washed away, and seabirds crying whose race had perished from the earth.

Elvishness is a kind of beauty, then, or even the essence of all beauty. That does not mean that *only* Elves are beautiful, nor that Hobbiton does not have a beauty of its own that differs from that of Rivendell or Lothlórien. Beauty is everywhere. But within earthly beauty, and more in some places and things than others, is a certain elusive quality that Tolkien tried to "refine," if you like, within the figure of Elvishness.

It is a sense of freedom, of a yearned-for infinity. It is something like coming home, but only at the end of a long journey. In a word, I suppose, it is the glimpse of *transcendence*, of what it might mean to go beyond all limitation, outside time itself perhaps, into a place where beauty converges and commingles with goodness and truth.

The longing for transcendent beauty is associated with a sense of melancholy, of infinite distance or separation, because we are far from home. Tolkien associates this especially with starlight, with music, and with the sound of water. Elvish art is concerned mainly with memory, and therefore tends to be somewhat nostalgic or wistful. As time goes by, the Elves are increasingly filled with memory; when time comes to an end, memory, it seems, is all they will have left. Even if "for them memory is more like the waking world than to a dream," as Gimli remarks on leaving Lothlórien, the fact that the yearning and love of the Elves is for *this world*, which is passing away, can be seen as tragic. Their existence is bound up with the created world they contemplate, and with the "sub-creativity" they exercise in accord with the gifts they have been given.

What Tolkien is ultimately concerned with is what he calls the "ennoblement" of the human race, and we can see now that this must imply both a theory of sanctity and a theory of beauty. Elvishness when mingled with humanity "ennobles" us because the Elves are our link back to the first Light, and their presence in our "bloodstream" (i.e., as an element in our nature) enables us to recall the Light that shone in the eyes of those who lived in Valinor before ever the moon rose or the sun dawned.

This light of "art undivorced from reason" is the light of *original participation*. It is the light that bathed the world fresh from the hand of the Creator, when "God saw that it was good." A sensitivity to this light, or a memory of it, is what attracts us to the Elves. Without this yearning for the light, for the beautiful, it would never be possible for us to attain the new, more conscious participation or state of communion that Barfield and Tolkien both, in their different ways, anticipated. That state of communion, Tolkien believed, was finally attained and made possible in Christ, through the gift of the Holy Spirit. Unlike the art of the Elves, Christian art is consequently able to celebrate and express the overcoming of the infinite distance between heaven and earth. (The work of Fra Angelico, for example, is radiant with the glory of heaven shining through earthly forms.)[30]

Men seek in the future what Elves seek in the past. But the love of beauty, for what is first given and taken from us by time, is a necessary part of our nature, if we are to be able to receive the light when it returns, if we are to recognize the Author of our existence when "the morning star rises in our hearts" (2 Pet. 1:19). In that sense the infusion of an Elvish spirit into humanity means to Tolkien the awakening of a divine discontent, an *eros* for the transcendent, which Christianity must always presuppose and rely upon. Without it, our spirits could not be receptive: they would be hard and closed, where they should be liquid and open.

Coming Home

> "Elves, sir! I would dearly love to see *them*. Couldn't you take me to see Elves, sir, when you go?'

The thread of Elvishness is wound into human nature by the marriages of Beren and Lúthien, Tuor and Idril, Eärendil and Elwing. Finally the marriage of Aragorn and Arwen sets the scene for the Age of Men, in the later stages of which we are now living. In Minas Tirith the White Tree blooms again, and "all the stars flowered in the sky."

Tolkien's body lies beside his wife's in the graveyard at Wolvercote, just north of Oxford, under a stone marked at his request with the names of Beren and Lúthien. The romance of these great heroes of the First Age is a poetic visualization of

Tolkien's own spiritual and psychological autobiography, ending with a journey into the unknown world of death.

If the story of Beren and Lúthien was so important to Tolkien that he engraved it on his tomb, it seems likely that Beren and Lúthien were for him the primary "archetypes" of Man and Elf respectively. The fact that one is male and the other female suggests that he placed in the Elves qualities that he (perhaps sentimentally) associated very largely with women: delicacy, creativity, musicality, beauty, unfailing memory, profound wisdom, lasting fidelity. If this is true, the masculine-feminine dynamic that some critics have failed to find in Tolkien's work is central to the story and to the whole cycle of stories, though in a disguised fashion. It is explored through the historical relationships of Elves and Men, "entwined" as they are through several key instances of intermarriage blessed by the gods. The love of beauty, which Tolkien symbolizes as a love of Elves and of Faërie—and therefore, as he explains, a love of enchantment, of imagination, of creativity—is intimately related to the love that exists between man and woman. In Tolkien's own life this makes absolute sense, for his creative writing begins at the time of his love affair with Edith, and is deeply bound up with her and the children to whom he read so many of the stories.

We note also that for all the high epic poetry, the center of *The Lord of the Rings* is not in Gondor; it is in the Shire, firmly rooted in the domestic. It is there that we must look for the final integration of Elvishness into human nature, within the romance as a whole. And this is what we find.

In one of his letters, Tolkien writes that the "chief hero" of *The Lord of the Rings* is not Aragorn. It is not even Frodo. It is the unpretentious gardener, Sam Gamgee (L 131). Sam appears to the reader, at least at first, to be little more than a Sancho Panza to Frodo's Don Quixote. Yet precisely because

Frodo is so elevated beyond the common life of the hobbits, it is Sam who is the truer incarnation of the Shire, and most deeply rooted in its soil. Sam's growth to maturity and the healing of the Shire go hand in hand. The story identifies this double process with Sam's winning of the hand of the girl he loves, and the book ends not with Aragorn's coronation, or with Frodo's departure into the West, but with his own return home to a loving wife and family.

> And he went on, and there was yellow light, and fire within; and the evening meal was ready, and he was expected. And Rose drew him in, and set him in his chair, and put little Elanor upon his lap.
>
> He drew a deep breath.
>
> "Well, I'm back," he said.

The story as a whole is concerned with "the ennoblement (or sanctification) of the humble" (L 181). Sam is the humblest of hobbits, a servant without ambitions—except perhaps to see Elves and Oliphaunts and eventually to have a bit of a garden of his own. For him to leave the Shire out of love for Frodo involves a great sacrifice. In a sense, he has to sacrifice the Shire itself—consciously so when he sees the threat to it in Galadriel's mirror but still determines to go on. It is fidelity to Frodo that remains his guiding star throughout. The plans of the Wise and the fate of Middle-earth are never his concern. He only knows he has to do his bit and help his master, however hopeless the task may seem. At a crucial moment in Mordor he must carry the Ring-bearer and even the Ring itself.

Sam moves from immature to mature innocence; and finally, back in his own sphere, the gardener and healer of gardens becomes a "king"—or at least a mayor. In fact, the Appendices tells us that he was elected mayor of the Shire no less than seven times, and it is to him that King Elessar will entrust the Star of the Dúnedain, which once represented the crown of the North Kingdom.

Sam's strength is not in the "ironmongery" he brings back from Gondor or his skill with a sword. It lies in the gift of healing that he bears from Galadriel: the box of blessed earth from her own orchard. Like Aragorn he has the power to heal his land of the hurts of war, and it is by this healing power that a true king is known, whether in Gondor or in Arnor. In Tolkien's intention, Sam is therefore paired with Aragorn as an "heir of Elendil," the archetypal Elf-friend.

Aragorn is not the only great hero with whom Sam is paired, at a level just below the surface of the text. As they wait to be engulfed in the ruin of Mount Doom, Sam sighs to Frodo,

> "What a tale we have been in, Mr. Frodo, haven't we? I wish I could hear it told! Do you think they'll say: *Now comes the story of Nine-Fingered Frodo and the Ring of Doom*? And then everyone will hush, like we did, when in Rivendell they told us the tale of Beren One-Hand and the Great Jewel. I wish I could hear it! And I wonder how it will go on after our part."

The reader is meant to identify Frodo with Beren, as Sam does. But an earlier exchange suggests a deeper intent on the author's part. After Gollum falls into the Fire, Sam catches sight of Frodo's bleeding hand.

> "Your poor hand!" he said. "And I have nothing to bind it with, or comfort it. I would have spared him a whole hand of mine rather. But he's gone now beyond recall, gone forever."

The desire to grasp is finally renounced; the grasping Shadow falls into the Fire and is forgiven. Frodo is marked by the loss of a finger—as Sauron lost a finger to Isildur—owing to his final (though in his case excusable) claiming of the Ring. Humble Sam may see Frodo as the great hero, but by that remark and the spirit it reveals it is Sam himself who is most closely conformed to Beren One-Hand—the great ancestor of Aragorn, and Tolkien's secret name for himself.

The story of Beren and Lúthien is echoed within *The Lord of the Rings* explicitly by the romance of Aragorn and Arwen. If I am right, it is echoed also by the long-postponed marriage of Samewise (Sam) to Rosie Cotton, which represents the "earthing" of the more distant epic marriages of Men and Elves. Of course, Rosie Cotton is not an Elven princess, any more than Tolkien's own Edith Bratt was. Nonetheless, it is a fact that when Sam names his first child (who, he says, takes after Rosie), he chooses to identify her with a flower that blooms only in Lothlórien. In *Sauron Defeated*, Christopher Tolkien tells us that his father's letter to Milton Waldman describing the projected Epilogue to *The Lord of the Rings* makes a point of referring to Elanor, "who by a strange gift has the looks and beauty of an elven-maid; in her all [Sam's] love and longing for elves is resolved and satisfied."[31]

Perhaps most profoundly of all, this final comment shows that for Tolkien the male-female dynamic is not, finally, a matter of a couple only, uniting in harmony the human with the Elvish elements in our nature, but of a *fruitful* couple; that is to say, of a couple that is open to being blessed with new life. It is not simply with his marriage to Rosie that Sam's *eros*—his love and longing for elves, the motivation for his journey—is fulfilled and blessed, but with the birth and growth within his home of Elanor and the other children.

The Healing of Arda

The Christian revelation does not enter explicitly into *The Lord of the Rings*. Tolkien reflected on many of the major themes that theologians are concerned with, but his thinking expressed itself there in imaginative mode—for the most part in the form of symbols and images.[32] Yet the secondary world he created was set in the past of our world. This gave him the opportunity to connect it with the primary world in a more direct way, if he could do so without straining the conception to the breaking point. That he attempted to do so is testimony to the seriousness with which he took his own project.

"The Debate of Finrod and Andreth" in the tenth volume of *The History of Middle-Earth*, which was at one time intended to form part of an Appendix to *The Silmarillion*, is probably the most theologically fascinating of all the posthumous works. It is also a powerful and emotionally moving piece of writing. Set in the First Age of the Sun before the meeting of Beren and Lúthien, the Debate takes place between an old wise-woman and Finrod, one of the brothers of Galadriel. It is accompanied by a detailed commentary and notes by Tolkien, which contains some of his most developed thinking about death and the soul, the relationship of Elves and Men, and the final destiny of both. We have already seen (in chapter 4) that death is one of the major concerns in Tolkien's writing. Here is the most explicit treatment of the subject in his fiction.

The dialogue is intense and poignant, for a reason that we discover only at the end: that Andreth in her youth fell in love with one of Finrod's brothers, Aegnor. While Aegnor remains ever young, and has departed from her, Andreth herself has faded and grown old. In attempting to console her in the course of their conversation, Finrod argues against Andreth's assumption that the aging and death of Men comes from Morgoth. He draws out from her the admission that in the distant past, Men may have committed some offense against the One God that led to the imposition of this penalty. Like all that comes from Eru, death would originally have been a beneficent gift, intended not for our hurt but for the perfection of our nature. Neither the body nor the death of the body were intended by him to be a burden, and nothing is evil in its beginning. (In line with Catholic teaching, Tolkien here is carefully countering any Gnostic or Manichaean tendency to view the physical body as an unmitigated evil.)

What he concludes is that the gift of death, which involves the separation of soul from body, was not intended to take this tragic form. Melkor's greatest success has been to turn it into an unnatural suffering, but in death before the Fall, rather than leaving it behind to rot, the soul of Man was to have taken the human body with it out of the whole realm of Arda, into eternity. This would have meant nothing less than a kind of *assumption into heaven.* The body would have been released from the limitations of time and space and healed from all the damage Melkor had wrought since the beginning in the substances of Arda.

Tolkien's speculation has a long history behind it. The theologians of the Catholic Church have all agreed that the separation of body and soul in Man is an "unnatural" state; that in some way the two components of human personality cannot be separated, and that they need each other. Since the most "natural" human state is (by theological definition) that which existed before the Fall, some have asked themselves whether Adam and Eve would have died at all, if they had not eaten the forbidden fruit. The Book of Genesis tells us that after the original sin, God expels man from the garden lest he "reach out his hand and take also from the tree of life, and eat, and live forever" (Gen. 3:22). This seems to imply that a tree of life had been placed in the garden for man to eat when the time was right, but that sin removed it beyond his reach. In other words, there was to have been a moment when death came to Man, but in that moment he would have eaten by God's permission from the tree of life. In the original plan, therefore, death would have occurred, but it would have taken a different form.

Melkor has turned death into a curse, but he has done more than that. By preventing the "assumption" of the human body Finrod believes he may have prevented the salvation of the Elves too. Being immortal, they will eventually have to face the death of Arda itself, when time itself comes to an end. In the original plan of Eru, the assumption of the bodies of Men would have implied the creation of a "new heavens and a new earth," an "Arda Remade" in which the Elves, perhaps, might have dwelt with Men, their deliverers, in an eternal present flowing with endless bliss. Now, in "Arda Marred" all seems to be forever lost.

Then Tolkien makes his boldest move yet. In the face of all the darkness he has painted, hovering on the edge of the darkest despair, through Finrod and Andreth he speaks to us of Hope (the "little sister," as the poet Charles Péguy called her, of Faith and Love). Finrod's word for this kind of hope is *Estel*, meaning trust in our deepest nature and first being, despite the apparent contradiction of what is known and experienced. Prompted by this definition, the woman recalls that there are some of her kindred who call themselves People of the Old Hope. They prophesy "that the One will himself enter into Arda, and heal Men and all the Marring from the beginning to the end." For her part, she cannot see how such a thing could happen. Finrod, however, replies:

> "If we are indeed the *Eruhin*, the Children of the One, then He will not suffer Himself to be deprived of His own, not by any Enemy, not even by ourselves. This is the last foundation of *Estel*, which we keep even when we contemplate the End: of all His designs the issue must be for His Children's joy."

Not even by ourselves. That is bold indeed, and a mystery we cannot fathom even in prophecy, if it suggests that somehow God will save us even from our own evil will to reject his love, yet without doing violence to our freedom.

Christians believe that Eru, the Creator, has fulfilled the Old Hope of Andreth's people and done precisely what is needed to heal Arda from within. In the Person of Jesus Christ he assumed human nature and suffered the worst Morgoth could throw at him. He allowed himself to be killed in the most violent way possible, experiencing the whole range of human suffering so that by filling it with his presence he could make it a bridge rather than a barrier between eternity and time. The fruit of that sacrifice can be seen already, the Church believes, in those most closely linked to Christ in time and space. The Virgin Mary, his mother, was assumed bodily into heaven at the moment of her death, just as (Tolkien suggests) Adam and Eve were intended to be in the beginning. In her the whole cosmos may find its way back to God. Perhaps the glory is greater now than it would have been, being won at such a cost. The hope of Arda is restored, and the Elves too may look forward with us to something "more than memory."

Tolkien was taking a great risk by inserting a prophecy of the Incarnation into his *legendarium*. Some readers may feel he has betrayed his principles, and that his religious beliefs are being allowed to intrude upon the story. Yet there is a great artistic integrity about the way it is done. Nothing is being forced: the characters are real within the secondary world, so much so that one feels great pity for Andreth and sympathy for Finrod. They do not step outside their own terms of reference within the secondary world.

What is happening here is that Tolkien is thinking through the Incarnation *from within his own subcreation*, almost as a way of testing its "consistency" with reality. I believe it passes the test.

The Secret Fire

Up to now, I have been speaking of light and of beauty. Light is the lifeblood of the world, of all things the most desirable, for it is the "luminous form of the beautiful."[33] It carries within itself the music of meaning. But the source of both light and beauty, according to Tolkien, is fire.[34]

The "secret fire" is Tolkien's term for the distinctive creative power of Eru. It is God's "secret," for only God can truly create *ex nihilo* (from nothing). For Tolkien the fire represents life, love, and creativity, the wisdom and love of God that burns at the heart of the world and sustains it in existence—it is a willed emanation from the creative energy of God's own self; it is the life of God shared with the world; it is the Holy Spirit, the "Giver of Life."

In Note 11 to the Commentary on the "Debate" in *Morgoth's Ring* he writes that the Flame Imperishable "appears to mean the Creative activity of Eru (in some sense distinct from or within Him), by which things could be given a 'real,' and independent (though derivative and created) existence." It refers "to the mystery of 'authorship,' by which the author, while remaining 'outside,' and independent of his work, also 'indwells,' in it, on its derivative plane, below that of his own being, as the source and guarantee of its being."

In view of the earlier discussion, we might call it the divine *eros*. We normally associate God with love in the sense of *agape,* or charity, and *eros* with the love of the sexes. But the word captures the passionate energy of God's love in a way that *agape* does not. The characteristic of *eros* is that it reaches out toward beauty: it is a response to beauty, or a recognition of it. In God's case it is the active *creation* of beauty. We find this wild, passionate, creative, and fiery love of God enshrined in the very heart of the Bible as the Song of Songs.

Eru sends forth into the void "the Flame Imperishable" to be the heart of the world. He has kindled the Ainur into reality with the same fire. This fire is that which Melkor seeks in the void, hoping to use it to create beings of his own, but he does not find it, "for it is with Ilúvatar." Thus it is that the Enemy cannot make, but only mar. He can imitate, distort, and copy, he can mock and corrupt, but he cannot truly create. Yet all his desire is bent on creation, and his inner torment is caused by this eternal frustration. He has become a flame, but a flame that gives more heat than light. He burns, which is to say he consumes instead of illuminates. His fire, compared to that of Eru/Ilúvatar, is shadow.

The ambiguity of the symbol "fire" comes into play in the following passage:

> The balrog reached the bridge. Gandalf stood in the middle of the span, leaning on the staff in his left hand, but in his other hand Glamdring gleamed, cold and white....
>
> "You cannot pass," he said. The orcs stood still, and a dead silence fell. "I am a servant of the Secret Fire, wielder of the flame of Anor. You cannot pass. The dark fire will not avail you, flame of Udûn. Go back to the Shadow! You cannot pass."[35]

The fire that is of God burns without consuming. Lesser fires may give light, and they may be used to give life and form to other creatures, but at the same time they consume the fuel on which they depend. Thus all lesser fires depend on God's gift of being, of fuel, of substance, continually renewed. The Enemy wishes not to depend on God, not to receive from him, but instead to be self-sufficient. That is not possible. Even the Balrog owes his existence not to Melkor, but to Ilúvatar.

The Book of Wisdom in the Old Testament describes something that appears very similar to Tolkien's "Secret Fire." Wisdom, or *Sophia,* is said to precede the creation of the world and to be placed at its very heart: "For she is a breath of the power of God, and a pure emanation of the glory of the Almighty: therefore nothing defiled gains entrance into her. For she is a reflection of eternal light: a spotless mirror of the working of God, and an image of his goodness" (Wisd. 7:25–26).[36]

Other biblical references to the Secret Fire are not hard to find. Adam and Eve are said to have been prevented from returning to the Garden of Eden by a "fiery sword." The Lord appears to Abraham like a fire walking between the divided animals when he makes the great Covenant with him and his descendants. The Prophet Elijah calls down fire from heaven to consume a sacrifice soaked in water when he restores the religion of Israel. Moses encounters God in the burning bush when he is told to lead the people out of Egypt. Later, after talking with God on the mountain, the face of Moses shines so brightly that it has to be veiled. He tells the people: "The Lord your God is a consuming fire" (Deut. 4:24). We see at the end of the Book of Exodus that God dwells in a luminous cloud, the manifestation of divine glory, which appears within the Tent that serves the Israelites as a Temple.

The New Testament—and the tradition of theological reflection based upon it—refines our understanding of the inner life of God yet further, for the Incarnation reveals God to be a Trinity of persons. And in Christian tradition it is the third person who is particularly identified with fire, for the Holy Spirit descends on the Apostles at Pentecost like "tongues of flame." Jesus tells his disciples, "I came to bring fire to the earth, and how I wish it were already kindled! I have a baptism with which to be baptized, and what stress I am under until it is completed!" (Luke 12:49).

In the New Testament, the Secret Fire is revealed to be not merely a force or a power, but a person in his own right. The Spirit is the personified Love that burns between the Father and Son, the Love that gives life and grace. No wonder Melkor sought it, and no wonder it could not be found, for it can be known only by those to whom it is given.

God dwells in "light inaccessible," yet in the New Testament that light emanates from and rests upon a living man. Peter, James, and John see their master clothed in this light and transfigured by it on Mount Tabor. "I am the light of the world," he tells the man born blind (John 9:5). It is the Incarnation that takes away the veil.

> Now the Lord is the Spirit, and where the Spirit of the Lord is, there is freedom. And all of us, with unveiled faces, seeing the glory of the Lord as though reflected in a mirror, are being transformed into the same image from one degree of glory to another; for this comes from the Lord, the Spirit. (2 Cor. 3:17–18)

The person who has seen the Son has seen the Father, and whoever has seen the Son has also seen the Holy Spirit. The eyes of faith become "eyes of fire," which see by virtue of a likeness to what is seen. The unity and distinction of the persons in God compose the secret of Christian sanctity, for we are called to personal unity in Christ, in which our own truest identity and mission will be revealed.

St. Bonaventure writes of the ecstasy of contemplation experienced by those who have followed the "mind's journey into God"; "This is mystical and most secret, which no one knows except him who receives it, no one receives except him who desires it, and no one desires except him who is penetrated to the marrow by the fire of the Holy Spirit, whom Christ sent into the world."

In the history of the Church we often find particular sanctity associated with a visible radiance, and even with flames. People rushed to put out a blaze in the forest of Umbria to find nothing but Saint Francis and Saint Clare talking together. The light of the Transfiguration shining from Saint Seraphim of Sarov in 1831 also filled a forest glade. Saint Philip Neri was praying in the catacombs of Rome when a great ball of fire descended into his chest. From that day onwards he emanated a warm glow even in winter, on which people could warm their hands, and when he died it was found that his heart had been strangely enlarged, displacing two of his ribs.

Tolkien shows us how to "think" with the imagination, using concrete images. Christianity, too, cannot dispense with *mythopoeia*. Theologians may speculate endlessly about the "divine energies" and whether these are notionally or really distinct from the divine essence, or about the act of Being (*esse*) and how it is participated by the world, or about the Holy Spirit and how he unites us in love with the Blessed Trinity, but in the end it is more important to kneel in adoration before an image of the Sacred Heart crowned with flames, or the Eucharist itself blazing out from the hands of the priest.

All love, all hope, all music finds a home with God, "who with divine freedom, but also with divine consistency, has fashioned for himself in his creation a body through which to reveal his glory."[37] Here in this body is the secret fire of our making and of our re-making, the luminous center of a new universe.

THE SECRET FIRE

I am the supreme fiery force
That kindles every spark of life;
What I have breathed on will never die,
I order the cycle of things in being;
Hovering round in sublime flight,
Wisdom lends it rhythmic beauty.
I am divine fiery life

Blazing over the full-repined grain;
I gleam in the reflection of the waters,
I burn in the sun and moon and stars,
In the breeze I have secret life
Animating all things and lending them cohesion.

I am life in all its abundance,
For I was not released from the rock of the ages
Nor did I bud from a branch
Nor spring from man's begetting:
In me is the root of life.
Spirit is the root which buds in the word
And God is the intelligible spirit.

—*St. Hildegard of Bingen*[38]

Chapter Seven

Tolkien's Achievement

Do not laugh! But once upon a time (my crest has long since fallen) I had a mind to make a body of more or less connected legend, ranging from the large and cosmogonic, to the level of romantic fairy-story—the larger founded on the lesser in contact with the earth, the lesser drawing splendor from the vast backcloths—which I could dedicate simply to: to England; to my country.... The cycles should be linked to a majestic whole and yet leave scope for other minds and hands, wielding paint and music and drama. Absurd.

—J. R. R. Tolkien to Milton Waldeman (L 131)

Absurd indeed. But we are not laughing. Tolkien, not alone, perhaps, but with the help of his son, achieved much of what he dreamed of achieving. The above extract is from a letter to a publisher in 1951 that was originally ten thousand words long and is not reproduced in full even in the published collection. The publication of *The Lord of the Rings* was hanging in the balance, and the letter was an attempt to show that it needed to appear together with *The Silmarillion*.

As we have already seen, Tolkien goes on to explain that the stories came first, growing in his mind as "given" things: "always I had the sense of recording what was already 'there,' somewhere: not of 'inventing.'" As we saw, *The Hobbit* was originally unrelated: he did not know at first that it belonged to the cycle. "But it proved to be the discovery of the completion of the whole, its mode of descent to earth, and merging into 'history.'" Thus *The Hobbit, The Lord of the Rings,* and *The*

141

Silmarillion, expanded now to include a host of other stories and fragments in *The History of Middle-Earth*, provide us with an immense mythological tapestry woven of many threads, taken from the legends of Northern Europe and elsewhere. The connection with "England" remains, though not in the way he had earlier envisaged.

We know from *The History of Middle-Earth*, particularly *The Book of Lost Tales* (pre-1920), that his mythology was in part an attempt to explain the "Elvishness" of England. The great city of Avallónë (Avalon, which of course enters into the tales of Arthur) stands on the coast of the Lonely Isle (Tol Eressëa), an island like a great ship, on which Ulmo drew the Elves across the sea, anchoring it eventually near the coast of Aman. In Tolkien's original conception this was to have been England itself, before it was invaded and disfigured by Men. The Elvish city of Kortirion was none other than Warwick (where Tolkien and Edith were married). The wistful atmosphere of the early Tales is concentrated in a couple of important and rather beautiful poems: "The Cottage of Lost Play" and "Kortirion among the Trees." But as time went by, in Tolkien's imagination England moved eastward (to somewhere in Beleriand and perhaps later Eriador), while the Lonely Isle floated westward. The Undying Lands retreated before him, becoming ever more remote, eventually being removed from the earth completely.

The direct "historical" links between England and Elvendom may have become tenuous, but in another way, as I have tried to show throughout this book, Tolkien succeeded in uncovering the Elvishness he had sensed buried deep within the languages and folklore of England, and expressed this in a mythological creation of enormous subtlety, power, and versatility.

It is often assumed by Christians that when God became Man, he fulfilled the ancient prophecies and thereby made all mythology redundant. Henceforth all mythological thinking would be something of a relapse back into superstition and ignorance. The sun had risen; the shadows were banished. But Tolkien is saying something different. A sun that does not cast shadows in broad daylight would be no sun at all. In the Epilogue to his essay "On Fairy-Stories" he writes:

> Redeemed Man is still man. Story, fantasy, still go on, and should go on. The Evangelium has not abrogated legends; it has hallowed them, especially the "happy ending." The Christian still has to work, with mind as well as body, to suffer, hope, and die; but he may now perceive that all his bents and faculties have a purpose, which can be redeemed. So great is the bounty with which he has been treated that he may now, perhaps, fairly dare to guess that in Fantasy he may actually assist in the effoliation and multiple enrichment of creation.

Tolkien thus stands with the rest of the Inklings and those who believe that Christianity does not abolish *mythopoeia* or poetic knowledge, but makes possible a new era of "baptized mythology," mythology that is no longer religion but "fairytale," an indispensable poetic evocation of a great mystery that is still unfolding within the world. "Art has been verified. God is the Lord, of angels, and of men—and of elves. Legend and history have met and fused." Christ may have come, but "the end is not yet." When it does come, even then there will be no end to the making of stories and of music.

The highest function of the fairy-tale, Tolkien tells us, is found in the sudden miraculous "turn," the grace of deliverance, the *eucatastrophe* or happy ending. This is not escapist, because it does not deny sorrow and failure, and indeed "the possibility of these is necessary to the joy of deliverance." But it denies *universal or final* defeat, by giving a taste or echo of victory, the final victory of Eru, who incorporates with his infinite creativity and foresight even evil into his design. Evil does not cease to be evil and must never be deliberately chosen; but it can never conquer the Good, which shines more brightly the more it is engulfed in darkness.

> It is the mark of the good fairy-story, of the higher or more complete kind, that however wild its events, however fantastic or terrible the adventures, it can give to the child or man that hears it, when the "turn" comes, a catch of the breath, a beat and lifting of the heart, near to (or accompanied by) tears, as keen as that given by any form of literary art, and having a peculiar quality.

This "turn" cannot be produced by doctrinal statement alone, no matter how true this is. It cannot be evoked in this way, because it essentially involves a moment of perception, which as we have seen is imaginative perception, or a seeing beyond the surface of things into their ultimate meaning. It is evoked by poetry that comes fresh from experience, rather than the kind of prose that delivers experience at second-hand. (That is why when Julian of Norwich says to us, "All shall be well, and all shall be well, and every manner of thing shall be well," we are moved to believe in a way that we are not when confronted by a more banal statement, such as, "Don't worry, everything will be okay.")

"There is a place called 'heaven' where the good here unfinished is completed, and where the stories yet unwritten, and the hopes unfulfilled, are continued" (L 45). The stories that we have received from Tolkien through his son are incomplete, and no doubt themselves only a pale and imperfect shadow of what he was striving to bring into the world. We may hope to see and hear them completed by the author in *Arda Healed.* Nevertheless, even as they stand, Tolkien's tree of tales forms a worthy enough backdrop to the one true fairy-tale, which is the tale of the Incarnation. For those who, despite having heard the word "Christianity," have never been introduced to the Gospel in a way that makes sense to them (or indeed, that does anything other than depress them!), reading Tolkien may be a revelation in itself. It may enable them to "hear" that Gospel as if for the first time, as the earth-shattering surprise it truly is—a surprise even to the gods who made the music before time.

In this book I have explored some of the reasons why Tolkien is one of the great spiritual writers of our time—of the age that dawned in the trenches of the First World War and today finds the shadows lengthening with the war on terrorism. He explored the human meaning of loss and death; which is what gives heroism, whether Christian or Pagan, its poignancy. The symbolic and interior struggle of Good with Evil, of virtue against temptation and weakness, of tradition against corruption and treachery, are represented realistically enough in the *legendarium* for us to be justified in seeing these works as a vehicle of great wisdom born of experience and suffering.

For Tolkien *did* suffer, as all do who live in such times, both personally and vicariously through a sensitivity to others. He was a man of his times, a product of modernity; yet at the same time, through faith, hope, and love, he transcended his times. His writing is dark—darker than his critics realize—yet it is suffused with the hope (*Estel*) that we need to find in ourselves if we are to carry on without turning back.

> "The brave things in the old tales and songs, Mr. Frodo: adventures, as I used to call them. I used to think that they were things the wonderful folk of the stories went out and

looked for, because they wanted them, because they were exciting and life was a bit dull, a kind of sport, as you might say. But that's not the way of it with the tales that really mattered, or the ones that stay in the mind. Folk seem to have been just landed in them, usually—their paths were laid that way, as you put it. But I expect they had lots of chances, like us, of turning back, only they didn't."

Sam first enters the tale by his ears, as Gandalf hoists him through the window at Bag End and "punishes" him for eavesdropping on the story of the Ring by sending him to Mordor with Frodo. Like Sam, we enter the story by listening, fascinated, to the Tale of the Ring. We find, like him, that once we are inside such a tale, it is difficult to escape, for our lives have been changed. We know the peril that threatens us, a darkness that encompasses the light. We realize that we are called to some form of service, so that the light may not perish from the earth. It is our knowledge of a light and a beauty worth defending that inspires heroism—even the heroism of hobbits, inspired to risk their lives by their love of the homely beauty of the Shire.

And it is the glimpse of a light and beauty, which in a sense does not need defending, that consoles the hero in his quest, and brings him peace of heart in the midst of his struggle. Deep within Mordor, looking up at the sky,

> Sam saw a white star twinkle for a while. The beauty of it smote his heart, as he looked up out of the forsaken land, and hope returned to him. For like a shaft, clear and cold, the thought pierced him that in the end the Shadow was only a small and passing thing: there was light and high beauty forever beyond its reach.

It is the glimpse of high Elvish beauty that inspires heroism, whether in the Third Age or this, the Seventh Age of the Sun.

Part Two

APPENDICES

Named "Appendices" in honor of J. R. R. Tolkien, the following short essays supplement the main text above and delve more deeply into certain topics that readers may find of interest.

Appendix One

An Archetypal Journey: Tolkien and Jung

We have seen that the quest of the Ring is presented from the start as a spiritual process that must be gone through, as much as it is a physical journey through hardship and danger. C. G. Jung's description of the therapeutic journey of the self can be helpful in describing some aspects of this process.

> There is in every word set down by the imaginative mind an awful undercurrent of meaning, and evidence and shadow upon it of the deep places out of which it has come. It is often obscure, often half-told...but, if we choose to dwell upon it and trace it, it will lead us always securely back to that metropolis of the soul's dominion. (John Ruskin)[39]

Timothy R. O'Neill's *The Individuated Hobbit* begins by giving an account of the rough outlines of Jung's theory, which, like Barfield's, is concerned with the evolution of consciousness. For Jung the psyche is divided between the personal conscious, the personal unconscious, and the collective unconscious. The latter is the repository of primordial images and predispositions termed archetypes, resembling the beds of rivers where the waters of life and common experience have dug deep channels. These archetypes, more or less charged with the psychic energy (*numen*) flowing through them, may reveal themselves and emerge into consciousness in the form of symbols, whether in dream or myth.

For Jung, the central archetypes are located in the strata of the psyche: consciousness is centered on an archetype called the *ego*, which acts as its controlling force under cover of the *persona* or social façade. The archetype of the persona, however, excludes all those emotions and images felt to be incompatible with civilized existence. These cluster around a deeper complex, below the level of consciousness, termed the *shadow*. This is a personification of the dark side of our nature. Depending on whether the individual is male or female, there will also be a series of repressed or undeveloped masculine and feminine characteristics (the ones our ego has less use for). These cluster around another deep archetype called the *animus* or *anima*. And hidden more deeply still is the archetype of the *self*, which forms a potential alternative center of the psyche as a whole, capable of integrating and unifying its various energies, and healing the fractures and imbalances between the various components.

persona
EGO
------------*threshold of consciousness*------------
shadow
animus/anima
SELF

Most of us are damaged and in need of healing. This can be accomplished by a process termed "individuation" by Jung. To put it crudely, the Self must be brought out of the depths and assume the position currently occupied by the ego. In fairy-tales, this process is often represented as a search for buried or captured treasure, and its retrieval through perils and darkness as the hero brings it through the shadow into the full light of consciousness.

> Our motivation is directed toward the ultimate joining of conscious and unconscious, and to the emergence of the Self as the new center of a balanced psyche. This is the final achievement to which these archetypal urges direct us. The Trickster in fairy tales may provide us with elusive clues; the Wise Old Man, archetype of wisdom and power, may guide us; the redeemer may sacrifice himself for the quest. Without the final goal of Self-realization, the symbols are only curiosities.[40]

A Jungian reads *The Lord of the Rings* as an account of "the individuation of the West." The real goal of the quest, according to O'Neill (pp. 50–51), is to heal the neurosis represented by the sinking of Númenor and the subsequent decay of its colonies in Middle-earth. O'Neill regards the very name that Tolkien has given to Atlantis in his mythos as being more than coincidentally related to Jung's term for psychic energy. "With the loss of Númenor the psyche of the West is suddenly unbalanced, the fleeting selfhood of that golden age lost beneath the waves (in the depths of the unconscious)."

The White Tree is one of the archetypes of the life process—the flow of *numen*.

> The withering of the tree is symptomatic of the centuries of decay and grief in Gondor, culminating in the death of the last king of the line of Anárion. In the veins of the King is the blood of the Lords of Númenor, the blood of Eärendil and Elwing, in which the opposites [Elves and Men] are united. (p. 50)

Thus the eventual "Return of the King" (who has been preserved in hope by the Dúnedain, the broken sword his symbol) is the return of the Self of the West as an integrating force. The Shire is Middle-earth in microcosm, so the Scouring of the Shire is a version of the same process of individuation in "Hobbit-mode," as it were.

Transformation always comes at a price. The healing of the soul of the West can come about only through facing, integrating, and dissolving the shadow, so that the Self can emerge into the light of consciousness. Sauron is the shadow of Middle-earth and of Aragorn as the true King. Gollum is the shadow of the hobbits: of Bilbo, Frodo, and Sam. Despised and outcast, he personifies the potential moral weakness and evil that lurk in the soul of the most humble. Sam frequently advises Frodo to kill him when he has the chance, and the hatred between them is one of the themes of their journey into the Land of Shadow.

There is probably a connection between the vulnerability of Sam to that hatred for a hobbit long ago corrupted by the Ring, and the evident vulnerability of the Shire to the corruption brought upon it by Saruman during the War of the Ring. The corruption of the Shire is made possible by the collaboration of a certain number of the hobbits themselves with the rule of the ruffians. Hobbiton can be healed of this moral weakness only by the reordering of the Hobbit soul; and Sam's soul is reordered and healed at the very end of the quest, on the side of Mount Doom, by first sparing and finally forgiving Gollum. The death of Gollum represents the facing and overcoming of the shadow both within and without.

It is easy to recognize Jungian archetypes in many of the other characters and symbols introduced by Tolkien into his narrative. Gandalf, pretty obviously, is the "wise old man" who features as guide to the psyche in the process of individuation. His staff is a traditional symbol of this hermeneutic function:

linking heaven and earth. In some mythologies it carries a serpent or tamed dragon, which in Gandalf's case is suggested by the fire that it can produce at his command and by its association with the conquest of Smaug in the earlier adventure. He is also a personification of the emerging Self of the West: his "greyness" purged in a confrontation with his "shadow" (the Balrog), he appears as Gandalf the White, the head of his Order. Aragorn, too, must pass through the shadow before he achieves mastery: he chooses the Paths of the Dead and leads the unresolved elements in the unconscious of the West (the dead Oath-Breakers) to a final act of expiation.

Galadriel features in the Jungian reading of *The Lord of the Rings* as a powerful positive symbol of the feminine archetype, and Shelob as the negative feminine within the Land of Shadow. Eowyn is another powerful female figure. The Jungian writer Helen Luke once described the King of the Ringwraiths accurately enough as "the ghost-like horror of the masculine spirit turned daemonic." That despair-inducing horror can be slain only by Eowyn as woman, and she must strike at its head, for it has no heart. She confronts the Ringwraith over the body of her fallen king, Théoden, representing chivalry and the old heroic virtues, which cannot avail against the Nazgûl. Eowyn strikes with the power of the heart, of personal devotion, of womanhood, assisted of course by Merry, the "child" that she as woman nurtures and protects.

The potential weakness of a Jungian interpretation of *The Lord of the Rings* emerges to view when O'Neill identifies the Ring of Power with the Jungian "Self"—surely almost an inversion of its true meaning. Concentrating on its perfect circular shape and color, he sees it as a positive image when Tolkien obviously intends the opposite. Tolkien's Ring suggests the power of the Enemy to deceive and to tempt. "All that is gold does not glitter," as the rhyme says of Aragorn; the Ring is not the Self but the false self, the self that binds and does not liberate. For O'Neill, Frodo's loss of the Ring explains why his own healing, his own self-realization, is precluded at the end of the book. Yet it is hard to see what Frodo could have done with the Ring that would not have turned him into another shadow.

The greatest flaw in the Jungian position from a Christian standpoint, and certainly from Tolkien's, is to regard God as what O'Neill calls "an image projected by the psyche." This leads him to omit the moral dimensions of the quest. Spirit transcends psyche: the Christian understanding of our moral life depends upon this distinction being made correctly. Morality is more than psychodynamics.

Jacques Maritain writes about the relationship of the unconscious and the spirit in his *Creative Intuition*:

> Reason does not only consist of its conscious logical tools and manifestations, nor does the will consist only of its deliberate conscious determinations. Far beneath the sunlit surface thronged with explicit concepts and judgments, words and expressed resolutions or movements of the will, are the sources of knowledge and creativity, of love and supra-sensuous desires, hidden in the primordial translucid night of the intimate vitality of the soul. Thus it is that we must recognize the existence of an unconscious or preconscious that pertains to the spiritual powers of the human soul and to the inner abyss of personal freedom, and of the personal thirst and striving for knowing and seeing, grasping, and expressing: a spiritual or musical unconscious which is specifically different from the automatic or deaf unconscious.[41]

By referring to the "deaf" unconscious, Maritain means the Freudian unconscious, which consists of instinct and memory, complexes and repressed emotions. It is called "deaf" because it is unreceptive to the intellect. The spiritual or musical unconscious, on the other hand, is the seedbed of poetic knowledge and creative intuition. The distinction that Freud's disciple Jung made between the personal and the collective unconscious, according to Maritain, is something quite different again, which cuts across both. Each of Jung's two constructs may be part of Maritain's spiritual or his automatic unconscious, depending on whether they are considered to be turned toward the world of the spirit or the world of matter, the intellect or the animal in us. We need both, for we human beings are not angels or entirely material creatures.

Although Tolkien would not have put it this way, a purely psychological account of man ignores a vital dimension of our existence, namely, that in which we are able (with the help of divine grace) to transcend our biological and even psychological existence. This process—termed in the Christian tradition not individuation but divinization—involves an additional discernment, not just between the ego and the Self but between the Self and the false self. This path is not one of balancing the elements and forces of the psyche alone, for at the level of the spirit we are part of a greater whole even than that of the Self. The false self can only be distinguished once the Self has been found, and at that point we are powerless to achieve the quest without help that comes from beyond ourselves.

Appendix Two

Tolkien's Social Philosophy

The Shire has been described by critics as an "agrarian idyll," an impossible paradise based on childhood memories, bathed in the rosy glow of sentimental nostalgia. This is not at all fair. Even before its infiltration and corruption by Saruman, the Shire has its flaws. The small-mindedness of its inhabitants, the unpleasantness of the Sackville-Bagginses and Ted Sandyman, are not there merely for comic effect, but to inject a genuine note of realism from the primary world.

In 1943 Tolkien wrote: "My political opinions lean more and more to Anarchy (philosophically understood, meaning abolition of control not whiskered men with bombs)—or to 'unconstitutional' Monarchy" (L 52). Nor does he have much truck with the modern notion of the nation-state: "I would arrest anybody who uses the word 'state' (in any sense other than the inanimate realm of England and its inhabitants, a thing that has neither power, rights, nor mind); and after a chance of recantation, execute them if they remained obstinate!" Government, he adds, "is an abstract noun meaning the art and process of governing and it should be an offense to write it with a capital G or so as to refer to people."

The "half republic half aristocracy" of the Shire (L 183) has an elected mayor but seems to function most of the time well enough without government, and its police force of "Shirriffs" has very little to do—that is, until Saruman's influence is brought to bear. At that point Government with a capital G arrives with a vengeance. No political system as such is immune to corruption. "I am *not* a 'democrat,'" Tolkien wrote in 1956,

> only because 'humility' and equality are spiritual principles corrupted by the attempt to mechanize and formalize them, with the result that we get not universal smallness and humility, but universal greatness and pride, till some Orc gets hold of a ring of power—and then we get and are getting slavery. (L 186)

Tolkien was not optimistic about the prospects for a civilization that had taken the path of Saruman rather than that of Gandalf (see L 53).

These real-life political opinions, which lie behind his fictionalized portrayal of English country life in the Shire, place Tolkien within a tradition of Catholic social thought known as "Distributism," whose most eloquent exponents in the previous generation were Hilaire Belloc and Gilbert Keith Chesterton.[42] As far as I know, he never referred to the Distributists or aligned himself with their cause. Nevertheless, before the Second World War Distributism had been one of the two main Catholic movements in Britain basing itself upon the social teaching of the Church. Tolkien tended to avoid politics where he could, and refers to Chesterton mainly as a poet. Nevertheless, I cannot see any political "camp" that would have suited him better. He was certainly no "socialist" in any sense (see L 181). The other popular Catholic movement, the Catholic Social Guild, would have been more congenial to him, but after 1942 it was increasingly aligned with the Labour Party. In any case, Tolkien's work and interests lay elsewhere.

Distributists saw the family as the only solid basis for civil society and of any sustainable civilization. They believed in a society of households and were suspicious of top-down government. Power, they held, should be devolved to the lowest level compatible with a reasonable degree of order (the principle of "subsidiarity"). Social order flows from the natural bonds of friendship, co-operation, and family loyalty, within the context of a local culture possessing a strong sense of right and wrong. It cannot be imposed by force, and indeed force should never be employed except as a last resort and in self-defense.

The problem with modern Capitalism, in the opinion of the Distributists, was that there were not enough capitalists around: property and wealth had become concentrated in the hands of a few, reducing other people to the status of "wage slaves" (hence the title of Belloc's book on the subject, *The Servile State*). The result in Britain had been a pseudo-democracy that was really a disguised plutocracy: actual power lay with the employers and the managers, and political parties were largely being manipulated by these for their own ends, public opinion being handled by allied interests in the media.

Distributists thought the answer lay in the direction of wider ownership (*not* "public ownership"); meaning that measures should be taken to encourage small and family-run businesses, farmers, and local retailers, and to defend them against the larger conglomerates. Forcible redistribution of land, however—of the kind we have seen in Zimbabwe, for example—was not an option: it was completely against Distributist principles. One of the most basic of these principles was freedom: the whole point of the philosophy was to foster self-sufficiency, independence, and personal responsibility.

The Shire fits neatly into this tradition of social thought. It represents an agricultural, largely self-sufficient way of life, cut off from the rest of the world and happy to remain so, that was already almost dead in Tolkien's time, killed by new methods of transport and communication. It was a way of life founded on local tradition, which Chesterton once famously called "the democracy of the dead"—one shaped by our ancestors, not just by those who happened to be walking around. More importantly, perhaps, it was founded on a respect for nature and for the environment that we seem to have lost in the headlong rush for economic growth at all costs.

Appendix Three

The Shadow of King Arthur

When the Israelites first demanded a king, Samuel told them in no uncertain words what they could expect.

> These will be the ways of the king who will reign over you: he will take your sons and appoint them to his chariots and to be his horsemen, and to run before his chariots.... He will take the best of your fields and vineyards and olive orchards and give them to his servants.... He will take the tenth of your flocks, and you shall be his slaves. And in that day you will cry out because of your king, whom you have chosen for yourselves; but the Lord will not answer you in that day. (1 Sam. 8:11–18)

The Lord told Samuel, "They have rejected me from being king over them" (1 Sam. 8:7).

Kingship is arguably the source of our most potent political mythology. The Israelites were not to be dissuaded from their decision "to be like other nations." And we find all that Samuel prophesied coming true. Yet God brings good out of evil, and in King David, only a generation later, he raises up a true hero: a king who is also a prophet, a poet, and a liberator. Builder-up of the great city Jerusalem, David is also a sinner. The privilege of creating a temple for the Lord is consequently reserved for his son Solomon—whose very name has become synonymous with wisdom, and the splendor of whose reign is legendary. "The king made silver as common in Jerusalem as stones, and he made cedars as numerous as the sycamores of the Shephelah" (1 Kings 10:27). Yet

Solomon, too, fell, and lower than his father ever did—with hundreds of women and foreign gods—until the Lord raised up enemies against him.

Each great king is able—or at least attempts—to draw on the mystique already accumulated around the names of his predecessors. We see it in the Caesars; we see it in those who would imitate them: Charlemagne, Napoleon, Hitler. We see it in the tsars and kings and princes of every country and region. In England we see it expressed in the legends of Arthur and the histories of Alfred; we see William the Conqueror, Richard the Lionheart, Henry VIII, and Elizabeth I aspiring to the same mantle, with varying degrees of success. The abuses of kingship are notorious. Yet even now (in some parts of the world) the institution survives. Americans often fail to understand its appeal—except in terms of the glamor that attaches to great entertainers like Elvis, or great political soap opera stars like the members of the Kennedy clan.

In keeping with the origins of their nation, the more archetypally American the hero, the more he (or she) is a lone individual set against a system or a wilderness. Even the five-minute heroes of the screen draw upon that mystique. Yet having a royal family at least enshrines the principle that society revolves around the family and not the individual.

G. K. Chesterton's *Ballad of the White Horse*, which Tolkien knew, is largely about the romance of kingship, in those far-off days when a king could be at the same time a hero. Such a king is not merely a lone individual, but the representative and guardian of a realm and a people, whether by virtue of the blood royal or by divine appointment (like Saul and David). Nevertheless, the hero, even when he is a king, must always be more than a cipher or a figurehead. The power of the archetype comes into its own when the king manages to combine possession of the cardinal virtues with the opportunity to act decisively at one of the turning points of history. Then archetype can serve personality, and personality the archetype: the king is worthy of the honor he receives. Such a monarch can become for each of us a living symbol not only of what binds us together in society, but of what we each aspire to become in our own circle.

Every nation has a legend or set of legends that help to define and enshrine its sense of identity and mission. For Chesterton, whose thought is so close to that of Tolkien in these matters, a national identity is shaped by the interplay of legend with landscape. Countries become beautiful, he thinks, by being loved—by being transformed in love by the imagination of those who live and die there. Those who have lived become part of the landscape and part of the legend. Graves and monuments are for visiting, and the shrine at the end of a pilgrimage provides a meeting place between earth and heaven that sanctifies the whole realm.

For Romantics such as Chesterton and Tolkien, imagination is an organ of perception, not merely of fancy. Mythology may be the only way that certain truths can find expression. But the imagination can also transmit a lie, a false perception. Tolkien writes of the way Hitler had corrupted the imagination of Europe: "Ruining, perverting, misapplying, and making forever accursed, that noble northern spirit, a supreme contribution to Europe, which I have ever loved, and tried to present in its true light" (L 45). The dark side of the imagination is to provide the irrational basis for all kinds of injustice and cruelty. In a fallen and corrupted world, our imagination is in desperate need of healing. It may still be an organ of perception, but the inner senses have light only through the moral organs of the soul.

The national legend of England was given form in the high Middle Ages by Geoffrey of Monmouth, Robert de Borron, the Cistercians, Malory, and a host of lesser storytellers. The whole edifice of Arthurian legend was based on fragmentary historical tales of a great chieftain who defended the remains of the Imperium from the barbarians after the protection of Rome was withdrawn. The Kingdom of Logres is, of course, more than a part (or even the whole) of what we now call Britain. It is our *inner kingdom*. Overthrown by human sin and weakness as soon as it was glimpsed on the stage of history, it was not destroyed but "withdrawn" into the imaginal landscape of Britain, just as Arthur himself was not killed on the field by Mordred but transported to the Island of Avalon.[43]

Avalon itself is often identified with Glastonbury Tor, which other legends link to the visit of St. Joseph of Arimathea with the Holy Grail. Joseph himself is symbolically linked by his cup and flowering staff to the two other Josephs of the Bible, in the Old and the New Testaments respectively. The national legend of England is thus a thoroughly "Christian" legend (in fact a bit too obvious a Christian allegory, Tolkien thought). Arthur's perennial mission is to render England receptive to the Blood of Christ, a receptivity of which the Grail is the emblem, and the flowering staff the result. (In John Boorman's film *Excalibur*, the land literally blossoms under the hooves of Arthur's knights.)

The Arthur story, like all Christian myths, conforms itself to its own supreme archetype, the story of Christ, which is both myth and history. Just as Christ gathered his twelve disciples, so Arthur gathered his knights. As Christ died on the cross before his kingdom could be realized on earth, so Logres ended in a field of blood and betrayal. But the perennial hope of healing and resurrection lives in the Grail, in the Eucharist, which may always be revealed to those who search for it. And as Christ will come again, so in him Arthur will one day restore the Kingdom of Logres.

I don't know whether Tolkien truly intended to rework the Arthurian legend of a Golden Age king, though it certainly formed part of the "leaf-mould" that nourished his own tale, and the parallels between them are numerous—even down to the fact that King Elessar is associated with a green stone (the Elfstone after which his house is named). For in Wolfram von Eschenbach's Arthurian tale *Parzifal*, the Holy Grail is formed out of a green stone that fell from Lucifer's crown when he was struck down by St. Michael. This possibly connects it also with the Silmaril taken from Morgoth's crown by the great hero Beren, an ancestor of Aragorn and the symbolic figure with whom Tolkien most identifies himself. But then, in Tolkien's fertile imagination all the tales and legends of Europe and the Middle East, from Gilgamesh to King Sheave, from Troy to Camelot, were gathered and their elements rearranged—a more accurate term might be "digested"—and transformed. Tracing these various influences on the author is an endless task, and one that Tolkien himself strongly discouraged. A story is to be *read*, he argued, not picked apart by critics and scholars.

Appendix Four

Friendship in
The Lord of the Rings

Through his fiction Tolkien explored at least sixteen key themes:

- Death and reincarnation
- Marriage and love
- Creation and creativity
- Myth and reality
- Virtues and vices / heroism and villainy
- Various kinds of wisdom
- Temptation and freedom
- Power and its corruption
- Providence and grace
- Beauty and nobility
- Technology and its perils
- Nature and the living world / Ecology and stewardship
- Social and political order / Small societies and localism
- The Fall and nostalgia for Paradise
- Language
- Friendship

The theme of *friendship* is an especially important link between Tolkien's own life and the stories he creates. For *The Lord of the Rings* is about the adventures of a "fellowship," that is, of a group of friends, whose love is tested and deepened by their experiences in the epic battle between good and evil. (The same is true of *The Hobbit*, of course, where the fellowship consists of Bilbo and the thirteen dwarves.) In the real or primary world, Tolkien's sense of friendship and his need for it was very deep, and his books would not have been written without the encouragement of the Inklings of Oxford, men such as C. S. Lewis, George Sayer, and Hugo Dyson. But the Inklings was only the last of a series of such groups to which he belonged or which he formed during his life, beginning with the "Tea Club and Barrovian Society" at King Edward's School in Birmingham.

In his earliest youth, as a child growing up in the woods and fields in Sarehole, playing with his younger brother, Hilary (who remained his closest friend throughout his life), Tolkien experienced the kind of close companionship that exists between brothers deprived of a father at an early age, and perhaps echoes of that very friendship come through in the relationship of Frodo and the younger hobbits in the pages of the story, where the early years of happiness in the English countryside were vividly evoked (the chapter "A Short Cut to Mushrooms" was based on an incident in Tolkien's own life). After their mother's early death in 1904, the two brothers became the wards of an Oratorian priest in Birmingham, Fr. Morgan, who must have seemed ancient to them, cloaked in the mysteries of the faith and possessed of great wisdom and power. In that unequal friendship one can perhaps catch a glimpse of Frodo's relationship with the old wizard Gandalf. Certainly Fr. Morgan was imbued with enormous authority over him, which Tolkien acknowledged by obediently keeping his distance from the girl he had fallen in love with, from the age of sixteen until his "coming of age" at twenty-one.

At school, the friendship between the four members of the TCBS has been described both by Humphrey Carpenter in his biography and by John Garth in his important study, *Tolkien and the Great War*. It seems that the four boys shared a sense of mission, believing that they had been called to bring a "new light" into the world, a light of beauty and poetry to conquer the darkness of materialism and the cult of power. In this respect they belonged to the tradition of English Romanticism we associate with William Blake, Samuel Taylor Coleridge, and William Morris. They came to full consciousness of this just on the eve of the First World War in which two of them (Robert Gilson and Geoffrey Smith) were soon to die. In the end, it was Tolkien who "carried the torch" for the group and fulfilled their mission—by writing *The Lord of the Rings*, with the encouragement of the Inklings. The fourth surviving schoolboy, Christopher Wiseman, remained a lifelong friend and a link back to that original conspiracy.

The War was the making of Tolkien the writer, just as it was of many "War Poets" (e.g., Rupert Brooke, Wilfred Owen, Siegfried Sassoon) who were moved by their experiences to turn them into art. It was the first "modern" war, in which vast numbers were killed by guns and tanks and poison gas. In the Battle of the Somme, often described as the worst disaster ever to befall the British Army, he saw the courage of the ordinary soldiers and fell in love with the true spirit of England, which he enshrined in the Shire. It was this courage and nobility of the humble that he tried to portray in Sam Gamgee. Sam and Frodo's struggle through the Dead Marshes in the approach to Mordor and their journey through the slag heaps of Mordor itself disguised as Orcs, are based on an all-too-vivid memory of those horrible months in the trenches.

Tolkien could see that the world of the English villages was threatened by exactly the cultural poisons that Saruman and his ruffians brought to the Shire. A "scouring" of this evil would be possible only if the English acquired the same virtues that Frodo, Sam, Merry, and Pippin brought back from their journey. The story aims to show how those virtues can be acquired. And it all starts with friendship—the love of Bilbo for Frodo, which enables him to pass on the Ring to him; Frodo's love for his fellow hobbits, which leads him to accept the need to leave the Shire for its own protection; and the love for Frodo, which causes Sam, Merry, and Pippin to stay by his side "through thick and thin." It is friendship—a love of the other for his own sake— that holds them together in the face of the challenges and trials that make them grow as people. By fighting together against great evils, they become capable of recognizing and standing up against the lesser evils and small corruptions of everyday life.

Just as Pippin and Merry rouse the Shire to resist the ruffians, so Tolkien wants us to become aware and to resist the evils that threaten our own generation. But no one can do it alone. Frodo needs the Fellowship to achieve the Quest. Friendship is the seed that grows into the heroism they acquire on their travels, and friendship is the key to their success at the end, when they find they are able to resist the ruffians. The lesson of Mordor has been well learned. Evil rules by fear and greed, and it is weaker than it realizes, because the enemy is divided each one against his neighbor, looking ever for his own advantage. Friendship is stronger, because individuals work together for a common cause. In the end, this is why Aragorn makes a more powerful king than Sauron. People follow him and support him because they love him.

The Council of Elrond is the moment when the Fellowship of the Ring is fully formed, and its mission to destroy the Ring in the fires of Mount Doom is there decided. (It is worth noting that Tolkien's name for the gathering of the TCBS from which he emerged with a renewed sense of purpose on the eve of War was "the Council of London.") The Fellowship is composed of nine members and five different races: Hobbits, Men, Elves, and Dwarves, with the wizard leading. The friendship seems most intense between pairs within the group: Frodo and Sam, Merry and Pippin, Legolas and Gimli, Aragorn and Gandalf. (Boromir is left somewhat floating as the odd man out, and so perhaps it is not surprising that he proves to be the weakest link.) The novel shows us that we begin to become heroes simply by being friends, by being loyal to each other through the trials that afflict us and holding tight to the things and people that are worthy of love.

Of all these friendships, in many ways that between Legolas and Gimli is the most intriguing. It overcomes an ages-long antipathy between the two races, whose great differences have led to suspicion and even hatred in the past. What they manage to prove is that friendship *does not depend on similarity*: people of completely different type and character may discover profound spiritual companionship in each other. Each comes to admire qualities in the other which he himself does not possess, and makes the effort to see the world from the other's point of view—to appreciate caves, in Legolas's case, and ancient spooky forests in the case of Gimli. In the end, we are told that at the passing of King Elessar, "Legolas built a gray ship in Ithilien, and sailed down Anduin and so over Sea; and with him, it is said, went Gimli the Dwarf," even to the Undying Lands where none of his race had ever set foot. The shared love that draws them together is that of Galadriel, who represents in the story a vision of beauty and wisdom untarnished by the Fall of the world and the passing of time.

The friendship between the members of the Fellowship, uniting as it does representatives of the various races of Middle-earth and hallowed by the gifts of Galadriel in Lothlórien, is the one force that can oppose the Darkness that afflicts the Third Age. Gifts, of course, are used to signify friendship, and true love is often described as a "gift of self." A gift, if sincerely given, is a kind of sacrament in which the Giver is represented, if not actually contained. We tend to keep such gifts, because they remind us of the person who gave them. Galadriel's gifts include the phial she gives to Frodo containing the light of the Morning and Evening Star—radiance from the Silmaril that Eärendil wears on his brow as he sails the heavens. The magical soil that she imparts to Samwise enables the healing of the earth, trees, and gardens of the Shire when they return home. Thus her gifts of friendship connect directly with a greater tapestry of story linking all their lives with the fate of Light and Life in Arda as a whole.

And what are we to make of the Ring, the One Ring, the Ring of Power, which Gollum (falsely) claims to have been a birthday present? As a symbol of friendship and its antithesis, the Ring could not be bettered. A golden ring has long served as a symbol of marriage, that closest form of friendship between the sexes: the binding of two into one. (In fact when Peter Jackson's movie was made, he used the wedding ring belonging to one of the production team as the model for the Ring of Power.) But just as evil is always an inverted mockery of the good, so the One Ring is an inverted mockery of the wedding ring signifying friendship. Sauron's Ring represents *the destruction, the antithesis, of friendship.*

This is apparent even before its true nature and origin is revealed. The Ring appears at first simply to be a magic ring that gives the wearer the gift of temporary invisibility. (Ironically, at the end of *The Hobbit* Bilbo returns from his adventures with a ring of invisibility only to find that his relatives would have been only too pleased if he had disappeared forever.) Gollum, Bilbo, and later Frodo find the Ring extremely useful. Gollum is able to use it to sneak up on his prey, while Bilbo and Frodo use it to avoid meeting the Sackville-Bagginses. Thus its main function is to enable the wearer to escape human contact, or personal relationship. We don't have to confront our enemies—they can't even see us. But even as such it has a corrupting effect, as Plato recognized in Book 2 of *The Republic* when he wrote the myth of Gyges of Lydia, a man who used a ring of invisibility to get away with anything he felt like doing. Before long Gyges with the help of his ring seduces the king's wife, kills the king, and takes over the kingdom. Plato uses the story to illustrate the difference between a just person and an unjust. He asks, do we act justly only because, if we don't, we may be found out? The truly just man is one who doesn't care what people think, he only wants to do the right thing. He will not be corrupted even by such a ring. Plato surmises that in this world his likely fate is to be whipped, chained, and crucified.

The Ring for Tolkien represents temptation, and specifically the temptation of power—the ability to force our own will on others and on the whole world. Tolkien, however, portrays a much more subtle temptation than Plato. A good person is corrupted by wanting to do good—but to do it on his own terms, believing he knows what is right for everyone else. In Christian terms, this is the opposite of humility, and especially of that humility before God that allows us to be led and shaped by him in order to achieve the real purpose for which we were created. To commit sin, in Christian terms, is to turn oneself away from one's fellow man and to destroy all possibility of real communion and communication with others. It is especially to turn away from God. It is therefore highly appropriate that one who makes himself invisible with the Ring has made himself *untouchable by the light,* which passes straight through him. There could be no better symbol of cutting oneself off both from others and from God. Paradoxically, though, when Frodo wears the Ring in Mordor, he does not feel invisible but feels naked in the dark in front of the great Eye of Sauron, the maker of the Ring. In the world of the Ring, there can be only one Will dominating all. It is a world without diversity, without personality, without freedom, without friendship.

Tolkien's story tells us among other things that we do not achieve anything great on our own; we all need each other. In particular we need to work with others in a friendship that binds us together across our natural differences. Together we are more than we can be alone. It is only the Dark Lord who thinks he can be greater without any rivals or friends. Tolkien disagrees both with the modern (Nietzschean) idea that a hero creates his own laws and values and with the premodern idea that our identity is determined by our people, our family, our tribe. Tolkien's view of the human person is such that it is determined neither entirely by ourselves nor by the collectivity to which we belong. To be most authentically myself is to be for others. It is by giving myself away that I find myself, along with my real destiny. And "greater love has no one than this, that one lay down his life for his friends" (John 15:13).

Appendix Five

Tolkien for Homeschoolers

Here are some thoughts on the possible use of *The Lord of the Rings* by homeschoolers.

The first thing is not to impose the book as a lesson, but to introduce it naturally at an early stage. Reading to a child every day, for example, as part of a bedtime ritual that can start as soon as the child is capable of gazing at a picture, is the foundation of everything. (You know this already.) In the case of Tolkien, there are books that can be used much earlier than *The Lord of the Rings*—his *Father Christmas Letters*, *Farmer Giles of Ham*, *Smith of Wootton Major*, and of course *The Hobbit*—as well as dozens of books by other authors, traditional folklore from all over the world, and many wonderful passages from the Bible. It doesn't matter that one is reading a book where the vocabulary is difficult—the meaning of a word can often be gleaned from context, although you should encourage questions and have a dictionary at hand.

When it comes to *The Lord of the Rings*, reading aloud continues to be important long after the child can read for himself. The sound of the words is important. Spend a bit of time getting the pronunciation of the Elvish words right (Tolkien's Appendices contain some guidance). The magic is in the language, as Tolkien would be the first to tell you. Once the story itself has come alive in the child's imagination, and perhaps after it has been read more than once, it becomes possible to explore a range of topics suggested by the book. Let's consider Language, Philosophy, Religion, Nature, Geography, History, Mythology, and Art.

173

First, *Language*. Many children try their hand at making up a secret language or code. Why not give them a helping hand, and use the game to teach them gradually about the basic rules and reasons for grammar and syntax, the possible use of word endings, and the shapes of letters? You could take a side-trip into the art of calligraphy, in which Tolkien was adept. Keep a good dictionary, and perhaps especially an etymological dictionary, to hand, and talk about the ways words have evolved. Often children's spelling and also word comprehension can be massively improved by paying a little attention to the composition of the words we use. It is, by the way, extremely helpful if a child can be taught to speak at least one other language while very young. It becomes much harder later on. Some children might like to try learning Elvish. Why not pick up a little Elvish, while mastering Spanish and Latin?

Philosophy. We are fortunate in having Peter Kreeft's excellent book, *The Philosophy of Tolkien*, to refer to. This will open up the whole world of philosophical thought to anyone who loves the story. (Children, of course, are as much philosophers as anyone else, and more so than many adults, whose ability to wonder and to question has long since atrophied.)

Religion. Tolkien's work is permeated with religious themes and "atmosphere." I don't think it would be a good idea to treat *The Lord of the Rings* as a mere religious allegory and attempt to decode it. Apart from anything else, this would be contrary to Tolkien's intention (remember his "cordial dislike" of allegory). Rather the way to connect the book with religion is by subtly directing attention to the plot, which illustrates the way Providence works in the real world, to the characters and how they develop virtues by struggling against temptations of various sorts, and to the moments when beauty reminds us of the transcendent. It should be possible also to talk about the way we find meaning in our own lives by answering the call to become a hero and following a quest of our own. Each of us is different, just as each member of the Fellowship of the Ring is different and has his own unique part to play. Our lives have a purpose, and we are part of a Great Story. But it might be better to let the book communicate these ideas in its own way and not turn them into a lesson plan.

Nature. Tolkien describes the natural word of Middle-earth with great love and attention to detail, so that one feels one has actually been there. You could examine his descriptions, study the flowers and plants and birds he refers to, and try to find places that remind you of parts of the book. Tolkien loved to go on walks in the countryside and was always dawdling to look at the flowers and trees (unlike his walking companion C. S. Lewis, who liked to walk faster). Try to do the same. Drawing or painting flowers and landscapes is the best way to get to know them.

Geography. Start with the maps. A fascination with maps and how to read and draw them will stand children in good stead later. Make similar maps of your own neighborhood or places you visit. Pore over atlases of the real world and try to see how Tolkien thought Middle-earth might have evolved into the Europe that we see today. Compare the maps of Middle-earth at the time of the War of the Ring with maps in some of Tolkien's other, posthumously published works, the tales of Beleriand and the other kingdoms in the earlier ages. Discuss how the forces of nature can gradually or suddenly reshape a landscape, raising or leveling mountains, drowning islands and plains, eroding new valleys. Convey something of the fascination of Dwarves with the "bones of the earth," and if possible take your children to see some "glittering caves."

History. The Lord of the Rings is about nothing if not history, and the "long defeat" of our exile from Eden and the yearning for Paradise that keeps us building civilizations, and our need for redemption (the "healing of Arda," as it is called in *The Silmarillion*). To explore the history of Middle-earth using the Appendices, creating time charts and writing little essays on each of the invented cultures might be a good way to get children interested in real history. With older kids you could look at what inspired Tolkien—the Anglo-Saxon culture, especially, and to some extent the Celtic. Connect Númenor with Atlantis, and compare with Plato's *Critias*.

Mythology. Here you have a golden opportunity to go on from *The Lord of the Rings* to the Norse and Icelandic sagas, and then to compare Tolkien's Valar with the pantheons of gods, not just in the Norse mythology but in Greek and Roman too. Read the tales of King Arthur and his knights and the legend of Troy, which have so many echoes in *The Lord of the Rings*. Compare the creation story in *The Silmarillion* with those of other mythological traditions. Reflect with older children on the relation of mythology to truth: these are not just failed attempts to explain the world scientifically; they also contain poetic insights and a kind of symbolic metaphysics.

Finally, *Art.* There are numerous examples of drawings and paintings in different styles inspired by Tolkien's writing, so it would be easy to look at these and develop an interesting art class. Tolkien himself illustrated many of the events and scenes in the books and even designed colorful heraldic designs for the different Elvish "houses" or families. Why not show these and encourage children to design similar symbols for their own family and friends? Move on from there to look at heraldry and coats of arms, used not only in feudal Europe but in the modern Church. This can help to awaken an appreciation of symbolism, as well as a sense of color and design (not to mention connecting back to history).

Appendix Six

Tolkien and Paganism

In this book I have taken the line that Tolkien's Catholicism is a "hidden presence" throughout *The Lord of the Rings* and the rest of the *legendarium*, and that the books contain an implicit theology and spirituality that is, in Christian terms, orthodox. However, I feel that more needs to be said on this point, since, as Catherine Madsen points out, Tolkien "was not a simple person, and how his Christianity worked on his storytelling is not a simple matter." Her remark is made in an essay called "Light from an Invisible Lamp," published in 2004 as the second chapter of Jane Chance's reader, *Tolkien and the Invention of Myth* (see Bibliography). I find it an impressive argument on behalf of Tolkien's "non-Christian" readers (the author herself is a convert to Judaism), and I want to respond to it in a way that may help to pull together some of the threads of this book for this new edition.

Catherine Madsen described her childhood reaction to *The Lord of the Rings*, with which I am sure many readers will resonate. "The book seemed to have far less to do with the New Testament than with the mountains I could see out my windows, but it moved me to religion. Indeed, having once goaded my parents in an argument into asking me, 'Well, what do you believe?' I ran to my room, brought out the three volumes, and presented them, saying, 'I believe *this*.' It was youthful extravagance; but I have never since been sure that it was false."

She goes on to say that for years she tried to find in Christianity what she had found in Tolkien, but to little avail. Commentators, she says, have "mined" the book for Christian content, but only succeeded in taking the enchantment out of it. She argues that while Tolkien's commitment to Catholic-Christianity is undeniable, his allegiance to the laws of the fairy-story is even deeper. He "did not intend his work to argue or illustrate or promulgate Christianity," and the Christian-seeming images in it are merely echoes: "If Elbereth owes something to the Virgin Mary—if one can never again hear the phrase *stella maris* without thinking *o menel aglar elenath*—it is her starriness that crosses over into Faërie, not her miraculous motherhood or her perpetual virginity."

Middle-earth in the Third Age, as we have seen, is a world almost devoid of formal or explicit acts of worship, apart from some invocations of Elbereth and a consoling or nostalgic awareness of great natural Powers and imperishable beauty in the almost unreachable West. Madsen writes, "Middle-earth is a monotheistic world—remotely; it has no theology, no covenant, and no religious instruction; it is full of beauty and wonder and even holiness, but not divinity. Even the reader need not worship anything to comprehend it. It is more important for the reader to love trees."

She says that the religious feeling of the book is therefore "curiously compatible with a secular cosmology." Moral decisions, such as the refusal to shoot an old man (Saruman) unawares and unchallenged, are made confidently but without invoking divine authority. More delicate acts of moral discernment (such as the refusal to kill Gollum even in "self-defense") are based on experience, on what the heart tells us, and on our stage of emotional development; while the sense of fate, of certain actions being "meant to happen" or of certain people being "chosen" for their task, is left "unnamed and inaccessible."

> Her analysis of the dénouement at Mount Doom is particularly telling. "As a child I felt that one of the crowning delights of the book—it would not be speaking too strongly to call it a eucatastrophe—was that Gollum got his Precious back: that his wickedness, his horrid speech, his murderous craving, and his pitiful existence were taken up into the center and solution of the story, and not by being redeemed but by being allowed to play themselves out.... Even sin is not wasted but rather woven into the pattern. In natural religion as in the Gospels, pity is a mystery at the heart of the world; but here it *encompasses* evil without either punishing or converting it. Gollum is the sacrificial goat that takes away the sins of the world. His life was its own punishment; his death is also his reward."

In *The Silmarillion*, as we have seen, God himself tells us that sin has been "woven into the pattern." And since Tolkien has set his story in a time before Moses, perhaps even before Noah, we should not look for redemption just yet.

Madsen's point that *The Lord of the Rings* is "curiously compatible with a secular cosmology" finds an echo in Nicholas Boyle's book *Sacred and Secular Scripture: A Catholic Approach to Literature* (DLT, 2004). But Boyle is arguing for a thoroughly Catholic reading of the novel. For him, part of its claim to greatness lies in the way Tolkien has created "a piece of popular literature that, in the spirit of G. K. Chesterton, reclaims the myth of England for Catholicism and uses that myth both to represent a more general twentieth-century experience of historical uprooting and to give new sense to the old tradition of the ascetic life lived in imitation of Christ and in the communion of saints." He has done that precisely by making the Hobbits "irreligious" in a peculiarly modern way. They do not even have a ritual moment of recollection before meals, as Faramir does.

> This setting in a world that does not yet know the Christian, or even the Jewish, revelation has the singular advantage that it also, as it were, prefigures a world so secularized that it has largely forgotten them: the archaic, or archaizing, features of the book are the metaphors for its ultra-modernity. The hobbits find themselves wandering through a landscape, both natural and human, that, metaphorically at least, is post-Christian.

Religion is represented by the old myths and stories, which to the hobbits gradually, through their adventures, begin to seem more real than the sheltered enclave of the Shire.

In the end, for Boyle Tolkien's work is probably more allegorical than the author would have wanted to admit:

> The planting of the fairy tree, which puts the Shire under the special protection of an elf queen, is something like the return of England, Mary's Dowry, to the Roman faith. The ultimate answer to our question, what are the hobbits? must then be that they are, at least by the end of the book, the representatives of a Catholic England which has resisted the temptation to secular modernity, in particular to Britishness, and has accepted its place within Christendom.

The Elves, then, represent both the magic of nature and the magic of Catholicism.

Even if we were to accept Boyle's interpretation, we could say that Tolkien's image is primarily eschatological: it looks forward to the Last Things and not to the achievement of a Golden Age on earth. At the most he offers a "golden moment" that does little more than arouse the yearning for something permanent.

Madsen also discusses the "fading" of the Elves and the sense of history as tragedy—Tolkien's refusal to offer easy healing or even comfort for the inevitable pain of this world. She finds the real hope, an entirely *this-worldly* hope, in "what Hobbits feel when they see elves, or the stars," or in the reader's appreciation of Tolkien's imagined landscapes, namely, the recovery of awakened senses, immediate attention, the capacity to see things "as we were meant to see them," as things new-minted and apart from ourselves, a "gratitude to other beings for their otherness." She herself regards this aspect of Tolkien's vision as the most compelling, but also the least Christian, comparing it to that of the Pagan writer John Cowper Powys (though one may find the same gratitude in the Christian Chesterton).

In a final coup de grâce against Catholic triumphalism she speaks of the importance of an escape from Christianity:

> its history, its accretions of theology which have put such a strain on both reason and kindness; its exclusiveness of doctrine which has caused such suffering to Pagans and heretics, and to Jews; the ugliness and want of intellect in most of its daily celebrations; and the burden of evangelism, which sets the individual Christian in a position of superiority that is always impossible to defend. The escape from all this into some state where the heart's reasons for believing can be remembered, some landscape illumined with a light for which our language has no name—perhaps not even the name of Jesus, so weighted down and so abused."

Though Tolkien would have disagreed with much of this, I have quoted Catherine Madsen's essay at such length because I find it both moving and helpful. Her remarks about theology and what she calls the "exclusiveness" of doctrine call for a much more extensive response than I can give here, though it is implicit in the rest of this book. They are consonant with some Pagan reactions to Tolkien's work, although Madsen is not herself a Pagan.

I am not concerned here with Satanism, which is a deliberate inversion of the value system of Christianity and therefore entirely parasitic upon it. Self-avowed Pagans tend not to believe in the Christian devil at all. Nor do they seem to approve of the sacrifices their ancient forebears might have offered: a modern Wiccan text, for example, reads: "Nor do I demand aught in sacrifice, for behold, my love is poured out upon the earth....I who am the beauty of the green earth, and the white moon among the stars, and the mystery of the waters, call unto thy soul." They are in that way (and others) a thoroughly *modern* religious movement, searching for a more participatory, shamanic relationship to the natural world, and they find aspects of that relationship in Tolkien. They point out that Tolkien draws most of the elements of his sub-creation (including many of the names of his characters) from the Norse and other ancient Pagan mythologies. They read *The Lord of the Rings*, then, as an essentially "Pagan" text.

Nothing prevents them from doing so, but they should know that what they regard as Pagan elements were viewed by the author himself—a well-informed and orthodox Catholic if anyone was—as entirely consistent with a Catholic worldview. At the very least, this must prompt a deeper exploration of the nature of Catholicism, along the lines I have tried to suggest in these pages. I want to argue that while it is undeniable that *The Lord of the Rings* has a huge appeal to modern Pagans, this is at least in part for good reasons. What these readers find evoked and celebrated in the book is worth celebrating: the enchantment of a natural world full of living presences, of stars associated with a benign femininity, of beauty and kindness allied with heroism, a freshness of vision giving rise to ineffable gratitude, a sense of wickedness integrated into some greater harmony. None of this is incompatible with Christianity, though historically many Christians have denied these very things. In that sense Tolkien is pointing us toward a richer and more beautiful conception of Christianity.

And so I can finally agree with Catherine Madsen's own conclusion in the essay already so extensively cited. "In *The Lord of the Rings* God is not shown forth, nor does he even speak, but acts in history with the greatest subtlety. He does not violate the laws of flesh or of food, but remains the last Other behind all otherness that may be loved. Those who are struck by this reticence will not turn to the Nicene Creed's formula *et incarnatus est* but to a more obscure and paradoxical Hebrew saying: *lo sh'mo bo sh'mo*, 'Where the Name is not uttered, there the Name is present.' For some thousand pages Tolkien refrained from taking the Lord's name in vain; invisible, it illuminates the whole."

Appendix Seven

The Beginning of Days

I have written already about some of the profound insights to be gleaned from Tolkien's account of the creation of the world, the Ainulindalë. But there is more to say.

> Creation was the greatest of all Revolutions. It was for that, as the ancient poet said, that the morning stars sang together; and the most modern poets, like the medieval poets, may descend very far from that height of realization and stray and stumble and seem distraught; but we shall know them for the Sons of God, when they are still shouting for joy. This is something much more mystical and absolute than any modern thing that is called optimism; for it is only rarely that we realize, like a vision of the heavens filled with a chorus of giants, the primeval duty of Praise. (G. K. Chesterton, *Chaucer*, p. 37)

Chesterton, Lewis, and Tolkien were united in appreciating the importance of mythology, folklore, and fairy-tales. In their own works they exemplified the power of *mythopoiea*, of poetic creativity, to communicate aspects of truth beyond the reach of the merely prosaic. Human creativity is for them a vital element in the divine image, and in every act of artistic creation we echo the divine creation of the world. How fascinating would it be, therefore, to reflect on this power of human language and art by composing a mythopoeic account of creation itself?

It may seem strange, even blasphemous, to set about comparing inspired Scripture with the work of a mere novelist and fantasist such as J. R. R. Tolkien, but I am not trying to set

184

the two texts on the same level. My starting point is the suggestion that mythopoeic thinking can be a way of expressing and exploring valid metaphysical intuitions. In the hands of a believing and devout Christian, moreover, like Tolkien or C. S. Lewis, a fairy-tale or mythological narrative may be a way of approaching revealed truths from a new and interesting angle.

Antoine Faivre, a prominent researcher into esoteric streams of thought, in his Afterword to a study of the mystic Jacob Boehme by the physicist Basarab Nicolescu (*Science, Meaning, and Evolution: The Cosmology of Jacob Boehme* [Parabola Books, 1991], p. 117), postulates a "commonality of nature between the human mind and the universe," such that Mind and Universe would be associated analogically, making the human mind "capable of interiorizing, then of refracting in the form of images and symbols, the very structures that 'maintain the universe in its inmost parts' [citing Goethe's *Faust*]." Another physicist, Michael Heller—a Catholic priest and winner of the 2008 Templeton Prize—has spoken of the "entanglement" of the human mind with the Mind of God, though he sees the structures that maintain the universe as mathematical in nature. But the point here is that images and symbols constructed by man—whether these be mathematical or mythic—can be supposed to reflect in some way the archetypes, and archetypal processes, of creation. Faivre writes that

> among the visionaries whose imagination presents itself directly as "creative," i.e. as capable of re-creating and, in a sense, of reproducing the archetypal configurations, the ones who go furthest are those who take the mythic as their basis. It becomes their foundation, the support of their meditations, their springboard and heuristic tool,

endowing their work with an aura of authenticity. The mythic, here, is a story experienced in images, a scenario organized in a triptych: first cosmology (even theogony) and anthropogony; then cosmology (or cosmography); and lastly eschatology.

I want to apply these words to Tolkien, since I believe that—in a stumbling, only partially conscious way, but in a way that bears comparison to more forthright mystics such as Boehme and Blake—he was engaged in an attempt not merely to entertain (for it was not the desire to earn a living by writing that was his primary motivation), but to discover the truth about the world and express it in a mythological narrative. His vision was clouded and his narrative never achieved its final form. Indeed as his son Christopher has shown, in later life, far from perfecting he was engaged in a process of dismantling and rationalizing it. But insofar as the vision did condense into a relatively stable form—the form of the published *Silmarillion*—we can glimpse his vision and discuss its implications.

Let us take a closer look at the stages of creation, then, according to Tolkien's "Elvish" Old Testament.

1. Eru makes first the Ainur, the Holy Ones, the off-spring of his thought. He speaks to them, propounding themes of music. The Ainur sing to him alone, each their own theme, gradually coming to understand each other and sing in harmony.

2. Eru proposes a new and mighty First Theme to all the Ainur together, which reduces them to amazed silence. He asks them to make their own music in harmony with this theme. They make the great Music, and he sits and listens.

3. Melkor tries to make his own music and the result is discord—a "raging storm, as of dark waters" around God's throne.

4. God stands (active), lifts his left hand, smiling, and a Second Theme arises. This theme too is defeated by Melkor.

5. Then God stands again, lifts his right hand, frowning ("his countenance was stern"), and begins a Third Theme, "deep and wide and beautiful, but slow and blended with an immeasurable sorrow, from which its beauty chiefly came," which is the Theme of the Children of Ilúvatar.

6. Melkor's theme continues alongside and intertwines with the Third Theme, trying to drown the divine Music, yet "its most triumphant notes were taken by the other and woven into its own most solemn pattern."

7. God stands for the third time, his face "terrible to behold," raises both hands, and brings the Music to an end with a single Chord, "deeper than the Abyss, higher than the Firmament, piercing as the light of the eye of Ilúvatar."

8. God leads the Ainur into the Void and shows them their Music in the form of light, of vision, rather than sound and hearing.

9. He then takes the vision away and they see Darkness for the first time.

10. God makes the world that was seen in vision, and prefigured in the Music, with the word "*Eä!* Let these things Be!"

11. The Ainur descend into the world at its beginning, to shape its history according to the Music they remember.

In Genesis, of course, the stages are very different. In the first account of creation, they are divided into six stages or "days." These are: (1) light and its separation from darkness; (2) the firmament of heaven; (3) land, sea, and vegetation; (4) sun, moon, and stars; (5) sea creatures and birds; (6) land animals and Man.

What points of contact can we find between these two accounts? Obviously, the overall message is the same: the One God has created all things good, and out of nothing. But is "Let there be light!" equivalent to the words "Let these things Be" (in which case Tolkien's is an account of what takes place *before* the stages described in Genesis), or is the creation of light found earlier, in Eru's manifestation of the world as a vision to the eyes of the Ainur (stage 8), which is followed by their first experience of darkness? I am not sure how far we can correlate the two accounts at a superficial level. More helpful might be to analyze the structure of Tolkien's account in its own terms to find its underlying logic.

After the initial "tuning up" stage, there are three themes proposed by God and a final chord that brings the Music to an end. Since, as Tolkien tells us in the letter to Milton Waldman, he is writing for a "mind that believes in the Blessed Trinity," the threefold structure of the Music is unlikely to be a coincidence, although this does not mean we must automatically identify each theme with the Father, Son, and Spirit in turn. In the subsequent history of Middle-earth, the *first theme* seems to correspond to the original harmony of creation before it is disturbed by Melkor (the Paradise of Arda illuminated by the great Pillars of Light, Illuin and Ormal). The *second theme* would correspond to the time of the Two Trees. The *third theme* sees the birth of the Elves under the

Stars, and of Men under the Sun and Moon (the Children of Ilúvatar). The *final chord* would then represent the bringing of the world to Judgment through the Incarnation and Passion of Christ.

Some may suspect a connection with the Kabbalah, given Tolkien's association of the Left Hand of God with his "smile" and the Right with his "sternness." For the Tree of the Sephiroth—a well-known conventional arrangement of the ten archetypal divine Names or Forces—has three columns. The central column is associated with the divine Will and Grace, the right-hand column with Mercy, and the left-hand with Severity ("sternness"). Right and left may be reversed depending on the orientation of the Tree. The importance of music and harmony in Tolkien's account would also fit with the Kabbalah, given the correspondence of the Sephiroth with the notes of a descending Octave, including the insertion of semitone intervals on the central column (some believe that the Kabbalah is related to the Pythagorean tradition, for which musical harmony is fundamental).

Even so, it is unlikely that Tolkien, as a devout Catholic, was consciously influenced by the Kabbalah or studied it in any detail. It is more likely that the parallels are either coincidental or due to the fact that the Kabbalah largely consists of a profound reflection on the same Scriptures that Tolkien was referring to. This might also explain another parallel with the Ainulindalë. The Kabbalah posits four distinct "levels" of the creation, or "worlds." These correspond to the four letters of the divine Name in Hebrew, and the four levels of the Pythagorean *Tetraktys*, as well as to Isaiah 43:7: "Everyone who is called by my name, whom I created for my glory, whom I formed and made." They may be correlated with Tolkien as follows: (1) Emanation, Azilut, Fire or the Glory of the Lord (Ezek. 1:27), with Tolkien's "Secret Fire"; (2) Creation, Beriah, with the Music of the Ainur; (3) Formation, Yezirah, with the Vision of Light; and finally (4) Making, Asiyyah, with the material world of being, into which certain of the Ainur descend at the beginning of time.

Whether or not Tolkien was familiar with the Kabbalah, he is likely to have come across many strands of medieval thought, including Christian Platonism. Take, for example, this account of the creation by Hugh of St. Victor, who is influenced by John the Scot and Dionysius the Areopagite, from the end of his *Didascalicon*:

> God, wishing to show his invisible Wisdom, drew its example in the mind of the rational creature [the Angels or Ainur], and next, by making the corporeal creature, showed the rational creature an external example of what it itself contained within.... For the angelic nature first existed in the divine Idea as a plan, and then afterwards it began to subsist in itself through creation. The other creatures, however, first existed in the Idea of God; next, they were made in the knowledge of the angels; and finally they began to subsist in themselves.

(Hugh distances himself from the Neoplatonic tradition partly by replacing the nation of the "world soul" as the animating force of nature with that of an "aethereal fire" or *ignis artifex* akin in some ways to Tolkien's "Secret Fire.") At any rate, it is safe to say that Tolkien's creation myth, like Hugh's account, belongs in the great tradition of Platonic speculation, and was intended to support and elucidate that of Genesis.

Louis Bouyer certainly thought as much. When he writes of the "thoughts" of God that are "spiritual persons" or angels, he might as well be speaking of Tolkien's Ainur (see *Cosmos: The World and the Glory of God* [St. Bede's Publications, 1988], pp. 195–96):

> Whatever use [the Church Fathers] may have made of all the terms coined by Plato to deal with the mysterious reality of the invisible world, which holds sway over the visible one and is known to us through it, the intelligible world (as they continued to designate it) was for them actually quite different from what it meant to the ancient Greeks.... The difference is a simple one: for Plato, the invisible world was one of ideas, whereas the invisible world Christians believe in is one of persons....
>
> As pointed out by Maximus the Confessor, among others, the difference between Plato's immutable ideas and these created persons is that the latter are God's eternal thoughts, forming the essentially one yet infinitely varied complex of his eternal Wisdom. Moreover they are all included in the Son, the living Word through whom God expresses himself. They are therefore living thoughts, for everything in the Word is life.... They make themselves unconditionally available to the divine call from the moment of their joint awakening to a distinct existence under the influence of the Spirit. All together, but each on its own behalf, they awaken to this distinct though unanimous existence, in adoration and praise of their creator....
>
> These created but blissful spirits are in the only begotten Son like countless sons of God, the *bene Elohim* of the Bible, the sons of dawn who sang together, according to Job, on the first morning of the universe. And this universe itself, as we know it from the outside, in its corporeal visibility, resonates with their singing, their *melos amoris,* set afire by the divine Spirit's *ignis amoris.*

One final point. In Tolkien's Ainulindalë, it is clear that the fall of Lucifer (Melkor, later termed Morgoth) took place before the creation of the physical world, and that the fallen angel "meddled in all that was done," in an attempt to claim it as his own, and thus the world was tainted from the outset. This may seem to lean toward the heretical Manichaean view that matter itself is evil and spiritual perfection consists in emancipating oneself from it forever, but this is not the case. The Catholic poet Paul Claudel (d. 1955) possessed a powerful poetic intuition into the meaning of Holy Scripture. In an essay called "Evil before Original Sin," he wrote:

> That the intervention of the Evil One played a part in the creation of the world is proved by the Gospel, which constantly refers to the devil as *Prince of this world*. St. Paul calls him *the power of darkness*. St. John tells us *that the whole world is beset by Evil*. And on Holy Saturday we are struck by the exorcisms that the priest performs above the *holy water*, as if to rid it of the bad element infused into it. Adam's sin merely aggravated but did not explain the general infestation of nature. Before Adam's sin there was physical evil and—as a necessary and integral part of the general plan—the suffering and death that the Apocalypse calls the supreme enemy, the first death, which symbolizes *the second death*. Thus God assumes exclusive responsibility for neither Behemoth and Leviathan nor the creation of the pests and mites, wolves and leprosy, tuberculosis and all the other fearfully insidious ills that beset and torture animal flesh. The Apocalypse tells us that the Lamb *was slain from the foundation of the world.* Thus there was something which had required the spilling of this redeeming blood since the creation of the world.

Claudel goes on to explain that the devil is by no means the author of his own existence, and adds (reminding us of the Ainulindalë's "he that attempteth this shall prove but mine instrument in the devising of things more wonderful, which he himself hath not imagined"): "If I were a painter and had a new Sistine Chapel as my commission, I should depict the Almighty as a wrestler battling it out with the Evil Spirit. But this match would not resemble the Greco-Roman struggles so much as Japanese judo, where the champion triumphs by making use of his opponent's own efforts."

Appendix Eight

Myths Transformed

After the publication of *The Lord of the Rings*, Tolkien became increasingly self-conscious about the work. Frequently he would have to explain it to the many admirers who wrote to him, and when doing so he tried to fill in details left vague or implicit in the published writings. By the end of the 1950s, his son writes, when he turned back to the Silmarillion papers, he realized he now had to "satisfy the requirements of a coherent theological and metaphysical system, rendered now more complex in its presentation by the supposition of obscure and conflicting elements in its roots and tradition." (I am quoting throughout this section from the part of *Morgoth's Ring* called "Myths Transformed.")

In particular, his respect for astronomy had led him to doubt his own mythological conception of a flat earth becoming round after the Fall of Númenor and populated well before the coming of the sun. He began to feel that the High Eldar living in Valinor, from whom these histories ultimately derived, must have known the "true," scientific formation of the solar system, even if their traditions were later confused by the Elves and Men who transcribed and transmitted them. But most seriously of all, he felt that he could not "make up [astronomically absurd] stories of that kind" in a world where everyone believes we live upon a spherical island in space. As he wrote tersely: "You cannot do this any more."

Christopher Tolkien comments: "It seems to me that he was devising—from within it—a fearful weapon against his own creation." It is sad to find Tolkien writing in his notes to himself that

> The Making of the Sun and Moon *must* occur long before the coming of the Elves; and *cannot* be made to be after the death of the Two Trees—if that occurred in any connexion with the sojourn of the Noldor in Valinor. The time allowed is too short. Neither could there be woods and flowers &c. on earth, if there had been no light since the overthrow of the Lamps!

The whole poetic conception of the mythology needed to be altered to accord with modern science. But that would have a knock-on effect, for even *The Lord of the Rings* was full of references to the earlier conception (such as the identity of Elrond's father with the planet Venus, the morning and evening star). As his son remarked, "the old structure was too comprehensive, too interlocked in all its parts, indeed its roots too deep, to withstand such a devastating surgery" (p. 383).

Yet in fact, Tolkien being Tolkien, the fussy, incomplete revisions to his myths are more interesting than one might have imagined. The sheer size of the universe is further developed, and the "centrality" of Arda is explained by the fact that it forms the appropriate stage setting for the great theological drama of the Children of God and the battle between Good and Evil. The sun is now intended from the start, and it is not kindled from the Golden Tree but hallowed by Varda with a "holy light" from Ilúvatar. Melkor desires the new light and ravishes the divine maiden who inhabits the sun. Thereafter the sun is marred, the maiden departs, and the original plan of the Valar is spoiled. The importance of the Two Trees in later history is now explained by the fact that they were kindled before the rape of the sun, so that both they and the Silmarils contain part of the light given to it by Ilúvatar.

The greatest problems Tolkien was wrestling with at this time seemed to concern not the sun, but the moon and the stars, and the difficulty of preserving elements of the myth in which the special relationship of the Elves to the stars is established. He played with the idea of dark volcanic mists hiding the sun, and with the construction of a dome that would protect Arda (or at least Valinor) from Melkor, inlaid by Varda with the patterns of the stars in the universe outside. Nothing really resolved it, and the revision was never carried through.

In *The Voyage of the Dawn Treader* by C. S. Lewis, the boy Eustace objects to being told that he is meeting a retired star in the guise of an old man: "In our world," he says, "a star is a huge ball of flaming gas." The old man replies, "Even in your world, my son, that is not what a star is but only what it is made of." I suspect that there is something truer in Tolkien's original mythological conception than anything that would have emerged from the later tinkering. But I may be wrong. Perhaps he was reaching for something he never attained, but could see in his mind's eye: a poetic revision of his cosmology that would assimilate modern science, and heal by a vision of beauty our culture that is so wounded by the severance of reason from imagination.

Appendix Nine

The Film of the Rings

Throughout this book there are scattered references to the three-part *Lord of the Rings* movie directed by Peter Jackson and released from 2001 to 2003. The two Peter Jackson movies of *The Hobbit* will be released in December 2012 and December 2013—too late for a review to be included before this book goes to press. But with the first three movies we already have much to go on. What shall we make of this remarkable filmic achievement? How faithful is it to the spirit of Tolkien's book?

Film critics and Tolkien fans, by and large, responded to the first three films with ecstatic praise. The most extreme example I saw was in a column that appeared in England's distinguished *Sunday Telegraph* newspaper. Kevin Myers, on February 1, 2004, drew attention to the failure of the Academy Awards panel to nominate the third part of *The Lord of the Rings* for any acting Oscars. True, it had received nominations in eleven other categories (and in fact it went on to win every single one of these Oscars), but to treat the movie merely as an unsurpassed technical achievement, according to Myers, was to miss its "monumental" significance as "probably the mightiest achievement in the entire history of cinema." The film is in fact "one of the greatest accomplishments of the human imagination," comparable only to such masterpieces as Beethoven's *Ninth Symphony*, Mozart's *Requiem,* or Shakespeare's *Hamlet.* In fact, he argued, "the films are a far greater artistic achievement than the books." "In their moral complexity, in their narrative lucidity, in the breadth of their vision and ambition, in the majesty of their execution, in the strength of their characterization and in their technical mastery, they have set unprecedented standards, ones indeed which may never be matched."

This praise is excessive, although I agree that the acting (by all the main cast members) deserves much greater recognition than the Film Academy was prepared to give it. However, I do not propose to compare the films with other great achievements of the cinema, let alone with the work of great artists such as Beethoven and Shakespeare. My concern here is merely to compare the film with the novel. If it is the supreme achievement of cinema to date, it is certainly not without flaws; it contains moments of pure cinematic genius, too numerous to list here, but alongside them many unnecessary crudities. Yet my conclusion will be that the spirit of the novel survives, more than many of us dared hope, into the movie. For this Christians will be inclined to thank the same unseen power who seems to have assisted Tolkien in developing his original conception.[44]

Since praise of the film is so ubiquitous and so extreme, I will begin with a few criticisms. Cate Blanchett may look like Galadriel, but her deliberately unsettling manner and vocal delivery is a disaster—in my view one of very few misjudged performances in the film. Elrond, too, is miscast. On the other hand, Orlando Bloom as Legolas makes up for a great deal. That is how an elf should be played—and even how he should probably look. In general the elves in the film appear somewhat too human and insipid, too smug and pompous, when compared to the strong yet ethereal, serious yet fun-loving Elves of Tolkien's masterpiece. We generally see them at night or in twilight, whereas Tolkien finds them often (and certainly in Lothlórien) in the broad light of day, a day indeed brighter and more colorful than anything in the world we know. However, the film's treatment of the Elves and the decision to associate them with mournful, haunting music is understandable if intended to convey more easily to a cinema audience (unfamiliar with the mythic context of the story) the fact that the time of the Elves in Middle-earth is coming to an end. There is a sense of the tragedy of history, of cosmic entropy itself, which is powerfully present in the movie, and perhaps it could not have been conveyed so effectively in any other way.

What of the Shire, that other "world within a world," close to the heart of Tolkien's vision? Bag End is realized to perfection. Hobbiton, on the other hand, is too Disneyesque for my taste. Probably only an English director could have understood quite how the balance of humor and seriousness was to be maintained in the case of the Shire. It was, after all, supposed to represent the world of "real life" within the novel. Tolkien's gentle caricatures of rural English folk were affectionate. Jackson's Shirelings are far too clownish, and some of the complexity of Tolkien's exploration of the English psyche is lost. This matters most at the end of the third movie, when the Scouring of the Shire is omitted completely, and the Travelers return to a homeland that has been completely unaffected by the great events "away down South."

To do this is to gut the story, but again, the director had his reasons for making this decision. Perhaps he felt that this was not to be a "mythology for England" any longer, but a mythology for the whole modern world. The "Shire" has lost something of its resonance: even in England, where the country villages Tolkien remembered from his childhood have long ago been swallowed up. Jackson obviously decided to concentrate primarily on the epic theme, and on the drama

surrounding Aragorn in particular, rather than trying to dupli-
cate every aspect of Tolkien's subtle interweaving of the epic
with the everyday. I cannot say that he was completely wrong
in this, for the movies could not have been made longer or
more complex than they are without losing all coherence. Yet
it may be that this decision contributed to a flaw that many
have noted in the films, which is the prolonged ending after
the main climax. In the novel, the many greetings and partings
that follow the denouement at the Black Gate and on Mount
Doom are woven together with a whole new drama: that of the
Hobbits' return, transformed by their experiences, and their
response to the corruption Saruman has wrought in the Shire.
Without that unexpected second climax, the last section of the
movie inevitably seems too drawn out, and lacking any confrontation with evil at home it appears a bit cloying.

The impression of sentimentality might have been avoided
in the editing of the film. Frodo's initial encounter with Gandalf did not quite work. When we first see Gandalf he laughs,
after trying to appear stern. One can see that his jollity is supposed to be bubbling up irrepressibly from within, but far from
appearing spontaneous, it appears forced. After the destruction of the Ring, and the staggering scenes of the destruction of
Mount Doom and the rescue by the eagles of Frodo and Sam,
the audience is not quite in the mood for a bedroom romp,
let alone one in slow motion. Some of this scene would have
been much better on the cutting-room floor, which with a
few other cuts would have left more space in the film for the
inclusion of important deleted scenes, such as the confrontation with Christopher Lee's excellent Saruman at Orthanc.
This scene, included in the extended version, contains several
important elements from the book, even if in the novel Saruman does not die at his own front door. Noticeably, when the

dialogue departs from Tolkien it begins to clunk—an example would be Saruman's "You are all going to *die!*" In fact, it has to be said that wherever the scriptwriters depart from Tolkien's magnificient prose the result is usually banal or melodramatic, and sometimes even ungrammatical.

As an Englishman, Tolkien would probably have hated the film's overt manipulation of the audience's emotions in a few places, even though he freely admitted weeping at times during the writing of the novel. One of those moments, of course, was omitted from the film entirely. It is when Gollum teeters on the brink of repentance, looking down on the sleeping Frodo as they climb the stairs to Cirith Ungol. Disturbed and insulted by Sam, he loses what may have been his one chance of salvation. The film substitutes for this the moving rejection by Frodo of Sam, at Gollum's instigation. Fortunately the salvation-drama is not completely lost. Earlier, during the passage of the Marshes, it becomes vividly clear that Frodo's trust in him, and his restoration of Gollum's original name, has indeed awakened what was left of the creature's conscience. The dialogue between Gollum and Sméagol is one of the most powerful and moving (as well as funniest) scenes in the film. In Jackson's new version of the story, it is Frodo's apparent betrayal of Gollum to Faramir that causes him (unbeknownst to Frodo) to set his own path toward an evil end, by confirming his earlier opinion that he can trust no one except himself.

As for Faramir, most of the fans of the novel find him miscast and mistreated by Jackson. In the novel, Tolkien tells us, he did not expect to find Faramir walking toward him in the woods of Ithilien. In fact this was the character he identified with the most in the whole of *The Lord of the Rings*. Faramir has a goodness and a nobility, a self-assuredness, equal to if less majestic than Aragorn's. He has the "air of Númenor" about him. In the film, the character is reworked to be more complex, more tormented (by the cruelty of his father), and more confused. Was this, then, a betrayal of the spirit of the novel? Well, we lose one fine person, but we gain another, of a slightly different kind. The Faramir of the film also rejects the temptation of the Ring, although for a time he thinks it his duty to take it to his father (and Frodo, it has to be said, has given him no strong argument to the contrary, since he has even lied to him concerning his "gangrel companion"). Faramir recognizes the importance of Frodo's mission only after observing his close encounter with a flying Nazgûl in Osgiliath—a scene that does not exist in the book, and which struck many viewers as rather odd, for it meant that Frodo had now shown the Ring at close quarters to the Ringwraiths, who in the circumstances and so close to Mordor might have been expected to make a more determined assault upon it. However, Faramir earns our love and respect during the third movie, becoming a fitting companion for the Lady Eowyn in the end (their romance is played out only in the extended version).

Aragorn himself is a marvel, and it is largely thanks to Viggo Mortenson's achievement in the role that the movie rises to the great heights it does. For, in a sense, while Frodo as the Ringbearer is the main hero of the film, along with Sam representing the reader projected into the story, the drama as a whole is presented by Jackson as taking place within the soul of Aragorn. The film is about a man achieving his destiny through self-mastery and service, and that man is Aragorn. He begins in a state of rejection, having renounced his claim to the kingship long before, fearful of his own weakness, which is the weakness of men and of his ancestor Isildur. The Ring would not be a problem if Isildur had not taken it for his own three thousand years before, against the advice of Elrond. Thus the

War of the Ring is Aragorn's war in a very personal sense, and not just because by it he may win the throne of Gondor. The definitive rejection of the temptation represented by the Ring is his task, even more than it is Frodo's.

Of course, Frodo bears the Ring for him, and Sam bears Frodo: this is why Aragorn's unexpected cry during the final charge at the Black Gate ("For Frodo!"), though Tolkien would never have written it (and by the way what happened to the horses they were riding?), can be seen as appropriate to the film. Jackson skillfully interweaves the struggle of Frodo and Sam up the side of Mount Doom with the events at the Black Gate, leaving no doubt that these are two halves of a single psychodrama. The combined will and self-sacrifice of Aragorn and Sam jointly carry Frodo to the threshold of his mission. Aragorn even lets Frodo and Sam go off together at the falls of Rauros, when he could easily have stopped them. When I first saw this, I thought it a mistake, and one that could have been easily avoided. But in fact it makes sense, as does the scene (again not present in the novel) where Aragorn closes Frodo's hand around the Ring. The Ring is his by right of conquest, as the heir of Isildur, and Frodo is taking it where he cannot, with his permission and support.

Aragorn's evolution from Ranger to King echoes the transformations that several of the main characters undergo, including the resurrection of Gandalf, which transforms him from Grey to White (signifying headship of the Order of the Istari). Aragorn's resurrection is symbolic: he walks the Paths of the Dead and is crowned at the hand of Gandalf once the final victory is secured. The force that impels Aragorn into his ultimate transformation is the love of Arwen. Here Jackson develops a theme that for Tolkien was at the heart of the story, though in the novel it is relegated to an Appendix. It was not simply in order to "bump up the love interest" or to find more lines for Liv Tyler (who does speak Elvish beautifully!) that the romance was moved center-stage. In Jackson's version, it is Arwen's faith in the destiny of her lover, and in her destiny with him as the mother of his child, that "mothers" him into existence as King. One of the most poignant scenes in the third movie is that in which Arwen, in the process of departing from Middle-earth, having accepted Aragorn's decision to break off the engagement (Jackson, not Tolkien), has a vision of their future child and rides back to confront and contradict her own father in Rivendell. The decision to link her destiny with Aragorn's thus confirmed, though in a much more complex way than Tolkien ever suggested, she becomes mortally ill, which forces Elrond to recognize the need to re-forge the shards of Narsil into Andúril, the Flame of the West. With the sword finally in his hand, knowing that the life of Arwen depends on the destruction of the Ring, Aragorn is at last able to overcome the fear of his own weakness that had previously been holding him back, and can summon the Dead to fight at his side in the battle for Minas Tirith.

This is not the Aragorn of the novel, but a more modern character, and even in victory he is less majestic, less identified with the formality and dignity of his office, than Tolkien envisaged—though I think he would have been stirred by Aragorn's magnificent address to the troops at the opening of the Black Gate ("Men of the West!"), with its implicit reference to the failures of Men in the early twenty-first century. Frodo too is more visibly childlike than the mature, fifty-year-old hobbit described in the book. Nevertheless the combination of the two works well, and the intimate link between their two missions can be sensed, even if it is not spelled out. Frodo is prepared to sacrifice himself. He does not expect to survive.

Aragorn must divert the Dark Lord's attention, and his armies, toward the Gate in order to give Frodo a chance of reaching Mount Doom; but in doing so, Aragorn must also throw his life, and that of his friends and soldiers, against overwhelming odds. An imprudent decision in the normal sense, but hardly irresponsible, since in it lies the only hope of true victory. (In the book, of course, he fights on even in the absence of hope, in the belief that Frodo has already been captured by the Dark Lord.) Aragorn's sacrifice, his preparedness to do the right thing at any cost, makes the destruction of the Ring on some spiritual level inevitable, even though its actual destruction is brought about less by Frodo (as everyone within the film at the time imagines) than by Gollum.

The struggle on the edge of the inferno is played out between Frodo, Gollum, and Sam. The Ring cannot be destroyed by an act of will. It is destroyed by apparent "accident," an accident that Jackson makes clear would not have occurred but for the many sacrifices that had been made along the way by Frodo and by each of the members of the Fellowship. In other words, the Ring is destroyed and the mission fulfilled not by some final heroic act of Frodo's, but by his living out of that mission on the road from Rivendell to Mordor. Every act of courage and fidelity and kindness along the way contributed to the destruction of the Ring and made it possible.

If you contrast that final moment on the bridge of the Sammath Naur with the climax of the *Matrix* film series, you can see the breadth and depth of Tolkien's moral vision compared to that of the Wachowski brothers, for whom the ultimate reason for action (according to Neo's final line) seems to be the arbitrary act of choice itself. The whole world of modern consumerism is founded on freedom of choice, but the moral life is founded on another concept: the power to *choose aright*. By yielding to temptation in the end, it could be argued that Frodo has exerted his "freedom of choice" in the modern sense; for he has simply chosen the Ring. But at that precise point, his actual moral power is taken from him. True freedom, in other words, consists in the power to *be*, which is a power that is spread over time. Thus Frodo's past self comes to the rescue of his present.

By prolonging Frodo's struggle with Gollum in the film, and making them *both* fall into the Abyss (though Frodo is subsequently saved by Sam in a ridiculous, clichéd cliff-hanging scene), Jackson's movie makes yet another point. Both Gollum and Frodo have been consumed with lust for the Ring. At that moment evil has taken possession of them both, and in the war of the one against the other the evil that unites them is cast into the Fire. The destruction of the Ring thus illustrates the great fact about evil that I have already noted in this book: that it is its own worst enemy. Earlier, we saw the Orcs in Minas Morgul killing each other, enabling Sam to rescue Frodo. Earlier still, the Orcs from Mordor and the Uruk-Hai from Isengard fell out among themselves ("Looks like meat's back on the menu, boys!"—a wonderful Jackson moment), enabling Merry and Pippin to escape into Fangorn.

It may seem odd that the Ring is presented all the way through the film as a great temptation to power, when all we know for *sure* that it can do is make one invisible and perhaps immortal. Frodo seems to acquire no special power when he claims the Ring: in fact, he evidently cannot even prevent Gollum from biting it off. Sauron, when he wore the Ring long before, was vulnerable to the blade that cut it from his hand. Perhaps even for him it is something of a delusion. In this, the strangest and least-remarked aspect of the film, Jackson seems to have been completely faithful to the novel. The Ring remains an enigma.

Perhaps one of the most important facts about the movie is this, that it revolves around a symbol, and a symbol that people seem able instantly to appreciate. The language of symbolism, and the ability to understand it cannot be entirely dead if so many have been able to understand the meaning of the Ring. Jackson's movie captures it well enough. The theme of the Machine against Nature is ever-present. He even manages to suggest the more spiritual sense of the Ring—the sense in which it is the ultimate source of inner corruption, the *diametric opposite of prayer*. In the film, Frodo spares Gollum even after the betrayal to Shelob, because he recognizes the power of the Ring in himself, and cannot bring himself to condemn the pathetic creature. As Frodo crouches admiringly over the Ring in the Dead Marshes, caressing it, we sense that he is fascinated by an image of perfection, of *himself* perfected, indestructible, endless. The Ring is the Ego, our idea of the self, that which is most precious to us, the one thing we think we cannot live without, the secret image of the soul into which we escape from reality. But at that moment Frodo suddenly becomes aware of Gollum, echoing his gestures, like a reflection of what he is becoming.

It is brilliant filmic moments like this that one remembers and treasures. Clearly, the main themes and spirit of Tolkien's novel have been respected, and most are reflected in some way in the film, despite its many flaws and failings. Not least of these is the theme of Hope (the Elvish *Estel*), associated with Aragorn in particular, interwoven with that of the inevitability of Death, the two coming together artfully in Gandalf's words to Pippin on the eve of battle and in the intensely beautiful song performed by Annie Lennox in the closing credits to which they look forward. (The other songs, and the whole tremendous musical score by Howard Shore, add another dimension to the film trilogy as a whole.) Even, and in a sense especially, the self-reflective quality is preserved of a story in which the central characters themselves recognize that they are in a story, yet without thereby undermining the "suspended disbelief" of the audience.

Living in remembrance of the past, celebrating it, rehearsing it, and recognizing that we are part of it, is an essential part of keeping any culture alive and growing—or of renewing it when it has almost failed. Thus when Aragorn is crowned King, he echoes the words of his forefather Elendil as he stepped on to dry land from the ruin of Númenor thousands of years before: "Out of the Great Sea to Middle-earth I am come. In this place will I abide, and my heirs, unto the ending of the world." (In the film, the actor sings the words to music he has himself composed, so intense is his identification with the part.)

From first to last, the civilizations of Middle-earth, whether these be the warrior-societies of Rohan and Gondor or the peaceable farming and trading communities that make up the Shire, are built up through remembrance and custom. It is a modern mistake to think that great personalities can grow without being rooted in the rich soil of the past, in the memory of great deeds and in fidelity to promises made across the generations. Civilization is founded on covenants that cannot be broken without consequence. The great army of the dead will fight to regain its honor in the service of the King.

The Lord of the Rings in its written form embodies a sense of reverence for the living whole to which we belong—the world of Nature, the world of Tradition, and the spiritual world of Providence. Modernity, in its negative aspect, is a rebellion against these three worlds. Remarkably enough, Peter Jackson's team managed to preserve all three in the making of the film trilogy. In this way, they have helped to remind us of something that had almost been lost to our civilization. We look to Jackson's *Hobbit* for more of the same.

Notes

Publisher details not in the Notes can be found in the Bibliography.

Introduction

1. C. S. Lewis, *Of This and Other Worlds*, ed. Walter Hooper (Collins, 1982), p. 112.

2. The *Letters* are referred to by number rather than page because of variations between British and American editions: "L 66" means Letter No. 66.

Chapter One: The Tree of Tales

3. A detailed study of the origins of Tolkien's writing may be found in John Garth, *Tolkien and the Great War*. As the title suggests, the book concentrates on the period of the First World War and traces the influence of that "first modern war" on the Silmarillion. The poem on Earendel was read to the Essay Club at Exeter College, Oxford, in November 1914. Quizzed by his friend G. B. Smith, he jots down some ideas about the story that lay behind the verse, and the result is instructive (Garth, p. 53): "Earendel's boat goes through North. Iceland. Greenland, and the wild islands: a mighty wind and crest of great wave carry him to hotter climes, to back of West Wind. Land of strange men, land of magic. The home of Night. The Spider. He escapes from the meshes of Night with a few comrades, sees a great mountain island and a golden city—wind blows him southward. Tree-men, Sun-dwellers, spices, fire-mountains, red sea: Mediterranean (loses his boat; travels afoot through wilds of Europe?) or Atlantic.... " Smith was a member of the "TCBS" (Tea Club and Barrovian Society). According to Smith, the mission of the Club was "to re-establish sanity, cleanliness, and the love of real and true beauty in everyone's breast" (Garth, p. 105). From 1915 Tolkien was working on a "Qenya Lexicon" in which he wrote that fairies came "to

teach men song and holiness": Garth points out that the TCBS had the same method and mission, a mission to which Tolkien remained faithful throughout his life (p. 107). It has even been suggested to me that there may be an echo of the early fellowship of the TCBS in the group of four Hobbits—Frodo, Sam, Merry, and Pippin—who form the core of the Fellowship of the Ring.

4. The "Notion Club Papers" appeared in Volume IX of *The History of Middle-Earth,* entitled *Sauron Defeated,* edited by Christopher Tolkien (HarperCollins, 1992). The five quotations from the story displayed below are from pages 195, 201–2, 206, 227, and 227, of the HarperCollins edition respectively.

Chapter Three: A Very Great Story

5. Humphrey Carpenter, *J. R. R. Tolkien: A Biography*, p. 89.
6. I owe this insight to Teresa Caldecott.
7. Carpenter, *J. R. R. Tolkien*, p. 73.
8. C. S. Lewis, *The Abolition of Man* (HarperCollins, 1978), p. 48.

Chapter Four: A Hidden Presence

9. Flannery O'Connor, *Mystery and Manners,* ed. Sally and Robert Fitzgerald (Farrar, Straus & Giroux, 1962), pp. 173, 175.
10. Dwight Longenecker, *Adventures in Orthodoxy: The Marvels of the Christian Creed and the Audacity of Belief* (Sophia Institute Press, 2003), p. 51.
11. John Saward, *Cradle of Redeeming Love: The Theology of the Christmas Mystery* (Ignatius Press, 2002), pp. 320–21.
12. For Tolkien's own speculations about what might have happened if Frodo had challenged Sauron with the Ring, and how Elrond and Galadriel might have been corrupted by it, see the end of L 246.
13. And mushrooms, for some reason known only to Hobbits!
14. In *The Silmarillion* there is reference to devil-worship among the later Númenoreans. In the earlier editions of this book I described this as a form of Paganism, but one of my readers writes, somewhat

reassuringly, that "Pagans don't believe in the devil or any personification of evil, and wouldn't worship one if there was one." For more on Paganism, see Appendix Six (also notes 19 and 34 below).

15. J.-P. de Caussade, *Abandonment to Divine Providence* (Doubleday Image, 1975), p. 48.

16. *Unfinished Tales* contains a very moving story of an unhappy marriage—that of the voyager Aldarion, who became the sixth king of Númenor, and his wife, Erendis.

17. He was also known as the Apostle of Confession, and indeed Tolkien would always try to receive the sacrament of reconciliation before Communion. For more on St. Philip, read Paul Türks, *Philip Neri: The Fire of Joy* (T. & T. Clark, 1995).

18. Thérèse died of tuberculosis, and her last months were spent in physical and spiritual agony, not even consoled by her faith, for that was taken away from her or buried so deep that she was no longer conscious of it. In more recent times, Mother Teresa of Calcutta was revealed after her death to have spent most of her life deprived of the experience of faith, despite the fact that all through this time she radiated joy and hope to those around her. Jesus forsaken on the cross experienced all of this, and worse. Without him, this suffering, in which the saints have a share, would be nothing but evil. In him and with him, however, it is redemptive. It too becomes a sacrament, something both human and divine, joining man and God.

General Note for Chapter Four: Lines of Descent and Main Characters in the Mythology

In the Age of the Stars, the first Kings of the Elves were **Ingwë** (of the Vanya), **Elwë**/Thingol and **Olwë** (of the Teleri), and **Finwë** (of the Noldor). Having been shown the bliss and safety that awaits them in Aman, they lead their peoples into the West. Elwë remains behind: he marries **Melian** (of the divine race of Maia) and settles in Middle-earth, where their daughter **Lúthien** is born.

The Noldor: In Aman, Finwë is slain when Morgoth steals the Silmarils. Finwë's sons are Fëanor (by Miriel), Fingolfin and Finarfin (by Indis). Fëanor in turn has seven sons, Fingolfin three (including Fingon and Turgon), and Finarfin five (including Finrod/Felagund and Galadriel). The Noldor return to Middle-earth out of the West in pursuit of the Silmarils.

Men: Men appear in the First Age of the Sun. The Edain or Elf-friends have three Houses: Beor, Hador, and Haleth. Beren, who later marries Lúthien the daughter of Thingol, with whom he recovers a Silmaril from Morgoth, comes of the House of Beor. Húrin and Huor, and their respective sons Túrin (the tragic hero) and Tuor (the human messenger of Ulmo), come from the intermarriage of the Second and Third Houses of the Edain.

The Half-Elven: The son of Beren and Lúthien is **Dior**, the first of the Half-Elven, the father of **Elwing**. Tuor marries **Idril**, the daughter of Turgon, King of Gondolin. Their child **Eärendil** marries Elwing, their sons being **Elrond** and **Elros** (the latter being appointed first king of Númenor). The two lines of descent from Eärendil are united again at the end of the Third Age by the marriage of **Arwen** the daughter of Elrond (her mother being the daughter of Galadriel) to **Aragorn** the descendent of Elros.

Chapter Five: Let These Things Be

19. Self-professed Pagan readers of the first edition of this book have objected to the implication that Pagans "worship" nature: they prefer the word "venerate." The contrast between Christianity and (modern) Paganism seems to lie rather in the conception of a transcendent God, where the emphasis in Paganism is on divine immanence. A balanced Christian perspective, of the kind represented by Tolkien, includes both transcendence and immanence. The best analysis of this relationship that I have seen is by Henri de Lubac. "Those who uphold immanence deny transcendence, whereas those who believe in transcendence do not deny immanence. Indeed, they grasp the idea of transcendence sufficiently to understand that it

necessarily implies immanence"—or, at least, they should. See H. de Lubac, *The Discovery of God* (William Eerdmans, 1996), p. 94.

20. G. K. Chesterton, *Saint Francis of Assisi*, in *The Collected Works of G. K. Chesterton*, vol. 2 (Ignatius Press, 1986), p. 44.

21. Verlyn Flieger, *Splintered Light: Logos and Language in Tolkien's World*, p. 59. She remarks that the word *Logos* (often translated "Word") "carried at one time far more meaning than it does today": it had the force of "*order, principle of organization, harmony*. It meant something very close to music in the Pythagorean sense."

22. Verlyn Flieger, *Splintered Light*, p. 59. "Be!" (*kun*) is also the first word of God to the creation according to the Koran (Surah 36:82).

23. Sam's remark in Lothlórien, "I feel as if I was *inside* a song, if you take my meaning," is more profound than he realizes. As we move from divine Idea, to angelic Music, to dynamic Image, to living Drama, we find the different human senses successively engaged: Mind, Hearing, Sight, and finally Touch, Smell, and Taste. This suggests connections with Patristic writings on the "spiritual senses." One might say that creation is a process of embodiment—preparing a body for the Lord. The Logos reflected in the waters makes an image. The Spirit breathing over the waters makes waves (music). The Fire in the water makes blood (life). The virtue of effective mythopoeic writing is that its meaning cannot be exhausted by a single prosaic summary.

24. J. H. Newman, *Parochial and Plain Sermons* (Ignatius Press, 1987), p. 453. In the creation story we find at the beginning of *The Silmarillion*, Tolkien makes a point of emphasizing the continued active involvement of the angels in the World, "which still the Ainur are shaping."

25. See Lawrence D. Goodall, "Of Universals, Angels, and Inklings," *Communio*, Fall 2002. Gergely Nagy's essay, "Saving the Myths: The Re-creation of Mythology in Plato and Tolkien" (in *Tolkien and the Reinvention of Myth*, ed. Jane Chance) provides a helpful discussion of Tolkien's Platonism. In the *Timaeus*, he points out, the Demiurge orders the world in accordance with the Forms, the

vision of which would be equivalent in this interpretation to the Ainur's experience "outside time" of the Music and the Light.

26. No account is given of the origin or nature of Tom Bombadil, though he is described as the oldest of living beings on the earth. Perhaps he is the spirit of nature, a Maia of Yavanna, incarnating the vigor of spring and summer. He originated in the Tolkien household long before *The Lord of the Rings*, as Humphrey Carpenter explains in his biography (p. 165). "Bombadil" was the name of a Dutch doll belonging to Michael that had to be rescued from the lavatory. A poem-cycle, "The Adventures of Tom Bombadil," was published in 1934. For Tolkien he was at first "the spirit of the (vanishing) Oxford and Berkshire countryside" (ibid.), and he evolved from there to become something deeper and stranger—a kind of "Green Man" (a mysterious archetype one often finds carved in medieval cathedrals and present in the story of Gawain and the Green Knight). For me he also represents the spirit of music, for he seems incapable of speaking prose: his words dance in a rhythm and shade into song, and "his songs are stronger songs." The Ring has no power over him, cannot even make him invisible, for "he is the master." He also reminds me irresistibly of the Fool—representing transcendent freedom, irresponsibility, and love—in Valentin Tomberg's interpretation of the Tarot (*Meditations on the Tarot: A Journey into Christian Hermeticism* [Amity House, 1985]).

27. But see "The Tale of Adanel" at the end of the Notes on the "Debate of Finrod and Andreth" (in *Morgoth's Ring*), where Andreth gives Finrod an account of the Fall as it has been passed down to her by the House of Hador.

28. The following from Cardinal Ratzinger (now Benedict XVI) might suffice to reassure us of Tolkien's orthodoxy on the point. "The teachers of the Church point to the fact that man was not shut out from the tree of life until after he had manoeuvred himself into a position that was not appropriate to him by eating from the tree of knowledge. He seized something that, if he lays claim to it of his own will, can only become his doom. The answer God gives to this

new situation is that man may not now also pick from the tree of life, since to be immortal in this condition would indeed be perdition. In that sense being barred from the tree of life, which is bound up with being destined to die, is a grace. If, in the form in which we now live, we had to live eternally, it really would not be a situation worth working toward" (Joseph Ratzinger, *God and the World: A Conversation with Peter Seewald* [Ignatius Press, 2002], p. 134).

29. *The tale of Beren and Lúthien is a tale of grace.* *The Children of Húrin* is a contrasting story of "dis-grace." Set only a few years after the adventure of Beren, it concerns the destiny of Túrin Turambar, who marries his sister unawares and slays himself in grief. The tragedy unfolds under the eyes of his father, the hero Húrin, captured by Morgoth in the Battle of Unnumbered Tears and fixed in a high seat for his torment, as Morgoth demonstrates his power to doom Húrin's family to darkness and despair. There are few glimmers of hope in the story: Tolkien confronts the reality of evil unflinchingly. It is only in the context of the *legendarium* as a whole that we see how rare moments of radiance, swiftly swallowed, may outweigh the dark. In the tale of Beren and Lúthien, with the glimpse it affords us of the power of love to move the heart of Death himself, we sense the distant promise of redemption.

In versions of *The Silmarillion* dated to around 1930, Tolkien clearly envisaged for Túrin a destiny beyond death more spectacular than that of any of his other heroes. For details see *The Shaping of Middle-Earth* (vol. 4 of *The History of Middle-Earth*, HarperCollins, 1986 and 1993), pp. 165 and 205. Túrin is resurrected for the final battle with Morgoth at the end of the world, after the destruction of the Sun and Moon. Fighting beside Tulkas and Fionwë, it is Túrin's black sword that deals the death blow to the Enemy (though how an Ainur can die is not explained), "and so shall the children of Húrin and all Men be avenged." After that, the three Silmarils are recovered from earth, sea, and sky, the two Trees rekindled, the mountains leveled and the dead awakened. Túrin, known as the *Conquerer of Fate*, and his sister-bride, however, are no longer numbered among mortals, and they go not to a fate beyond the world. What this might mean is left unclear, but it may mean that they have by-passed the normal destiny of Men and gone straight to what Christians call the Resurrection—to the "new heavens and the new earth." They are "named among the Gods." In other words, Tolkien has constructed Túrin's tragedy on earth in such a way as to make him take the brunt of Morgoth's wickedness. His resurrection for the final battle, then, enables him to perform an act of reparation, a final human contribution to the working out of the healing process initiated by the Incarnation.

Chapter Six: Behind the Stars

30. John Saward explores this in *The Beauty of Holiness and the Holiness of Beauty* (Ignatius Press, 1997).

31. See also the author's footnote to the chronology in Appendix B of *The Lord of the Rings*, where he preserves the reference to Elanor's elvish looks. The name Elanor itself is composed of the Elvish words for *star* and *sun*, reinforcing the connection to the central mystery of light in the *legendarium*.

32. The theologian Louis Bouyer, one of the founders (with Hans Urs von Balthasar and Joseph Ratzinger) of the international review *Communio*, had profound affinities with Tolkien, since he knew him well, visited him in Oxford, and appreciated the enormous theological importance of his mythopoeic writing. According to Bouyer, Tolkien understood better than anyone how the novelty of the Incarnation, far from abolishing myth, could stimulate the myth-making faculty. The old myths express an expectation, still confused, that the Gospel was to clarify and satisfy with its true story of God entering human history. Christian fairytales anticipate the "transfiguration of everything" that constitutes the supreme object of Christian hope. They put down the roots of hope to unheard-of depths. The new job of the poets since the Incarnation is no longer just to give us hints of paradise lost, but to show us the form of paradise regained. Bouyer's friendship with Tolkien is revealed in Michaël Devaux, *Tolkien: Les racines du légendaire* (Ad Solem, 2003). I owe this summary to Dr. Cyprian Blamires.

The extract above on pp. 191 from Louis Bouyer's book *Cosmos: The World and the Glory of God* (St. Bede's Publications, 1988) echoes important themes in *The Silmarillion*.

33. Hans Urs von Balthasar, *The Glory of the Lord*, vol. 1 (Ignatius Press, 1982), p. 153. Balthasar's book develops in full, I believe, the "theological aesthetics" that the Inklings were reaching for, or that is implied by their work.

34. I have naturally stressed the Catholic inspiration behind *The Lord of the Rings*. Only a small proportion of Tolkien's admirers, however, are Christian, let alone Catholic. Wherever he derived his ideas and images, they have an appeal and a resonance well beyond any single religious tradition. This is as it should be. Tolkien was reaching back to a time long before Christ and before the great "axial period" of the world religions five centuries before that. As we have seen, he did not hold with Max Müller's view that religion evolves from a primitive stage of mythology and superstition to a more conscious and scientific apprehension of the world. That view, expressed in the best-selling *Outline of History* by H. G. Wells and effectively demolished by G. K. Chesterton in *The Everlasting Man*, was anathema to the Inklings. Tolkien believed that Paganism contained much that anticipated and pointed toward the full truth that had been revealed in Jesus Christ. If he is correct, we would expect to find echoes of the concept of "secret fire" in many religions and cultures—and so we do. For example, Fire or "Agni" (in Latin *Ignis*) is one of the names of God in the ancient liturgical hymns known as the *Rg Veda*. The Hindu scholar Ananda Coomaraswamy (d. 1947) describes Agni as the giver of the Spirit (breath), a "formal light that is the cause of the being and becoming of all things" (*Coomaraswamy 2: Selected Papers, Metaphysics*, ed. Roger Lipsey [Princeton University Press, 1977], p. 191). He also points out an "equivalence of life, light, and sound" in the similar roots of the words for "to shine" and "to sound"—a connection present even in English when we speak of "bright" ideas and "brilliant" sayings (p. 193). Thus the shining of Agni is a kind of speaking, and the Angels which are his Rays make a harmony that lies behind all things: "And sundry sang, they brought

to mind the Great Chant, whereby they made the Sun to shine" (ibid., p. 195). All of this may remind us of Owen Barfield's discussion of the word "shine," summarized by Verlyn Flieger in *Splintered Light* (e.g., pp. 48 and 74).

35. The passage I have just quoted has caused endless discussion among fans of the book and of the movie. Is the secret fire the same as the "flame of Anor" or different? Some have thought that the latter is a reference to Gandalf's sword, Glamdring, which was once worn by King Turgon of Gondolin, but the word "Anor" is obscure. It seems to be a variant of the Quenya name of the sun, Anar (which would explain why it is found in the name of the "Tower of the Sun," Minas Anor, later renamed Minas Tirith or the Tower of Guard, and of the flower *elanor*, which Frodo translates as "sun-star"). In *Morgoth's Ring* (p. 44) Christopher Tolkien admits there is a puzzle about the word, for in some manuscripts Tolkien seemed to have used "Anar" to refer to *Eä*, or the World of Being. Despite this, it is reasonable to suppose that "flame of Anor" is indeed an ancient Elvish name for Glamdring referring to the brightness of the blade, a name that we surmise is known only to Gandalf (and perhaps the balrog, who could well have been one of those who attacked Gondolin).

36. This is not the place to delve into the many interpretations that have been offered of this passage and the biblical notion of Wisdom. For further theological illumination one might do well to turn again to Louis Bouyer, and particularly to his book *Cosmos: The World and the Glory of God* (St. Bede's Publications, 1988), pp. 188–93.

37. Hans Urs von Balthasar, *The Glory of the Lord*, vol. 1 (Ignatius Press, 1982), p. 441.

38. The poem is cited from Seyyed Hossein Nasr, *Religion and the Order of Nature* (Oxford University Press, 1996), p. 59. At the end of his famous book *A Brief History of Time,* the theoretical physicist Stephen W. Hawking repeated Einstein's question, "How much choice did God have in constructing the universe?" At that time Hawking was working toward a "quantum cosmology"—that is, the marriage of quantum mechanics and relativity theory. He believed that the universe might be "completely self-contained, with no singularities

or boundaries, and completely described by a unified theory." Such a universe would have no Big Bang, no point of origin. Nevertheless, he continued, "Even if there is only one possible unified theory, it is just a set of rules and equations. What is it that breathes fire into the equations and makes a universe for them to describe?" To this question both Hildegard and Tolkien had the answer.

Appendices

39. John Ruskin, cited in James S. Taylor, *Poetic Knowledge: The Recovery of Education* (State University of New York Press, 1998), p. 116.

40. Timothy R. O'Neill, *The Individuated Hobbit*, p. 37.

41. Jacques Maritain, *Creative Intuition in Art and Poetry* (Harvill Press, 1954), p. 94.

42. See G. K. Chesterton, *The Outline of Sanity* (IHS Press, 2001), and H. Belloc, *An Essay on the Restoration of Property* (IHS Press, 2002), which contain the most accessible introduction to the social philosophy of Distributism. The subject is extensively discussed in many issues of the *Chesterton Review*. See also *http://www.distributistreview.com* and *www.secondspring.co.uk/ economy*.

43. In Tolkien's *legendarium*, Avalon becomes "Avallónë," the Haven of the Eldar on Tol Eressëa, nearest to Valinor. In the earliest forms of the mythology, Tol Eressëa is actually Britain, although that notion was discarded later.

44. For a fascinating collection of commentaries on the film, see Croft, ed., *Tolkien on Film*.

Bibliography

Books by J. R. R. Tolkien

Only those books mentioned in the main text are listed.

The Hobbit, or There and Back Again (published 1937 by George Allen & Unwin, revised 1951 and 1966, and by HarperCollins in 1995).

The Lord of the Rings (published 1954, 1954, and 1955) in three volumes by George Allen & Unwin, and by HarperCollins in 1991).

Poems and Stories, including the essay "On Fairy-Stories" (published 1980 by George Allen & Unwin, and by HarperCollins in 2002 under the title *Tales from the Perilous Realm*).

The Silmarillion, edited by Christopher Tolkien (published 1977 by George Allen & Unwin, and by HarperCollins in 2001).

The Letters of J. R. R. Tolkien, edited by Humphrey Carpenter with the assistance of Christopher Tolkien (published 1981 by George Allen & Unwin, and by HarperCollins in 2006).

The History of Middle-Earth, vols. 1–12, edited by Christopher Tolkien (1983–96), especially vols. 1 and 2, *The Book of Lost Tales* (published 1983–84 by George Allen & Unwin, 2002 HarperCollins); vol. 5, *The Lost Road and Other Writings* (1987/2002), vol. 9, *Sauron Defeated* (HarperCollins, 1992); and vol. 10, *Morgoth's Ring* (1993/2002). Vol. 4, *The Shaping of Middle-Earth* (1986/2002), is of interest for the insights it gives into the evolution of *The Silmarillion*. It includes an important prophecy of the final battle with Morgoth at the end of the world (pp. 165, 205).

Unfinished Tales, edited by Christopher Tolkien (published 1980 by George Allen & Unwin, and by HarperCollins in 2001).

The Children of Húrin, edited by Christopher Tolkien (published 2007 by HarperCollins).

The Letters of J. R. R. Tolkien

The following letters in particular contain substantial material for the further exploration of Tolkien's oeuvre, its ramifications and significance—including its religious and spiritual dimension.

Letter 43 (see also 49). On women, marriage, chivalry and the Eucharist.

Letter 113. To Lewis, offering a rare insight into the friendship of the Inklings.

Letter 131. A detailed summary of his life's work.

Letter 142. In which he speaks of his Catholic inspiration.

Letters 144, 153–56. The metaphysical background, and answers to difficult questions.

Letter 163. His account to W. H. Auden of how he came to write the books.

Letter 181. About the quest and Frodo's "failure"; on Elves as artists.

Letter 183. A detailed response to Auden's review; on politics, Good and Evil.

Letter 186. The various underlying themes and meaning of *The Lord of the Rings.*

Letter 200. About the "gods" and their role in the story.

Letters 207, 210. Tolkien's hilarious comments on the film "treatment" proposed in 1957.

Letter 211–12. On the mythology and its purpose.

Letter 214. The traditions and social arrangements of Hobbits.

Letter 246. Frodo's "failure" and fate.

Letter 297. On names in *The Lord of the Rings,* their origins and meaning.

Letter 306. On the state of the Church after Vatican II.

Letter 310. On the meaning of life, written to a schoolgirl.

Further Reading

Bassham, Gregory, and Eric Bronson, eds. *The Lord of the Rings and Philosophy: One Book to Rule Them All.* Open Court, 2003.

Birzer, Bradley. *J. R. R. Tolkien's Sanctifying Myth: Understanding Middle-Earth.* ISI Books, 2002.

Boyd, Ian J., and Stratford Caldecott, eds. *A Hidden Presence: The Catholic Imagination of J. R. R. Tolkien.* Chesterton Press, 2003.

Caldecott, Stratford, and Thomas Honegger. *Tolkien's* The Lord of the Rings*: Sources of Inspiration.* Walking Tree Publishers, 2008.

Carpenter, Humphrey. *The Inklings: C. S. Lewis, J. R. R. Tolkien, Charles Williams, and Their Friends.* George Allen & Unwin, 1978.

———. *J. R. R. Tolkien: A Biography.* George Allen & Unwin, 1977.

Chance, Jane. *Tolkien's Art: A Mythology for England,* revised edition. University Press of Kentucky, 2001.

———, ed. *Tolkien and the Invention of Myth: A Reader.* University Press of Kentucky, 2004.

Croft, Janet Brennan, ed. *Tolkien on Film: Essays on Peter Jackson's* The Lord of the Rings. Mythopoeic Press, 2004.

Curry, Patrick. *Defending Middle-Earth: Tolkien, Myth, and Modernity.* Floris Books, 1999.

Flieger, Verlyn. *A Question of Time: J. R. R. Tolkien's Road to Faërie.* Kent State University Press, 1997.

———. *Splintered Light: Logos and Language in Tolkien's World,* revised edition. Kent State University Press, 2002.

———, and Carl F. Hostetter. *Tolkien's* Legendarium: *Essays on "The History of Middle-Earth."* Greenwood Press, 2000.

Garth, John. *Tolkien and the Great War: The Threshold of Middle-Earth.* HarperCollins and Houghton Mifflin, 2003.

Kreeft, Peter. *The Philosophy of Tolkien: The Worldview behind* The Lord of the Rings. Ignatius Press, 2005.

Lobdell, Jared, ed. *A Tolkien Compass.* Open Court, 1975.

O'Neill, Timothy R. *The Individuated Hobbit: Jung, Tolkien, and the Archetypes of Middle-Earth.* Houghton Mifflin, 1979.

Pearce, Joseph. *Tolkien: Man and Myth.* HarperCollins, 1998.

———, ed. *Tolkien: A Celebration.* HarperCollins, 1999.

Purtill, Richard. *J. R. R. Tolkien: Myth, Morality, and Religion.* Ignatius Press, 2003.

Rateliff, John D. *The History of the Hobbit.* HarperCollins, 2011.

Reynolds, Patricia, and Glen H. GoodKnight, eds. *Proceedings of the J. R. R. Tolkien Centenary Conference, Keble College 1992.* Tolkien Society/Mythopoeic Society, 1995.

Rutledge, Fleming. *The Battle for Middle-Earth: Tolkien's Divine Design in* The Lord of the Rings. Eerdmans, 2004.

Shippey, T. A. *J. R. R. Tolkien: Author of the Century.* HarperCollins, 2000.

———. *The Road to Middle-Earth.* HarperCollins, 1992.

Wood, Ralph C. *The Gospel according to Tolkien: Visions of the Kingdom in Middle-Earth.* Westminster John Knox Press, 2003.

Bibliographic details of other works cited that are not directly about Tolkien or his work will be found in the Notes or where they are cited in the text.

Online Resources

The Tolkien Society: *www.tolkiensociety.org*
The HarperCollins Tolkien website: *www.tolkien.co.uk*
The Encyclopedia of Arda: *www.glyphweb.com/arda*
The Mythopoeic Society: *www.mythsoc.org*

Sites Devoted to the Study of Tolkien's Invented Languages

www.elvish.org
www.uib.no/People/hnohf

Sites for the Most Prominent Tolkien Illustrators

www.tednasmith.com
www.john-howe.com
www.endicott-studio.com/gal/galalan.html

Verlyn Flieger's Website
www.mythus.com

Index